Can You Turn It Off?

A Diary of Psychic Awakening

ISBN: 978-1-60910-167-1

Printed in the United States of America.

Booklocker.com, Inc.
2010

Can You Turn It Off?

A Diary of Psychic Awakening

By Derek Calibre

For my friends:
I am ever grateful for your laughter, wisdom and guidance.

Every story in this book is true, from my own point of view. I changed the names of all the clients mentioned, and a few of the names of my friends as well. A couple of the readings described are compilations of separate readings. Some of the readings may have occurred on different dates than noted. I wrote the diary piecemeal over a period of six years. Once I began to understand the nature of the book that was emerging, I tailored some of the entries to help it all work as a whole.

Acknowledgements

For their help with this book, I am grateful to *Margaret Bendet, Vivienne Leheny, Austin O'Toole, Fleurette O'Toole, Colleen Joubert, Mary Savage, and Kelly Greenlee.*

YMCA song lyrics by Henri Belolo, Jacques Morali, Victor Willis

These are among the many books that have helped me understand my psychic ability:

Ask Your Angels by Alma Daniel, Timothy Wyllie, and Andrew Ramer
The Secret Language of Signs by Denise Linn
What A Coincidence! Understanding Synchronicity In Everyday Life by Susan M. Watkins
Creative Dream Analysis: A Guide to Self-Development by Rev. Father Gary K. Yamamoto
Ariadne's Clue – A Guide to the Symbols of Humankind by Anthony Stevens
Opening to Channel by Sanaya Roman and Duane Packer
The Nature of the Psyche by Jane Roberts
Medicine Cards by Jamie Sams and David Carson
Motherpeace Tarot by Karen Vogel and Vicky Noble
The Complete Book of Tarot Reversals by Mary Greer
The Tarot Handbook: Practical Applications of Ancient Visual Symbols by Angeles Arrien
Forward to Wilhelm's Book of Changes by C.G. Jung
Jung and Tarot by Sallie Nichols
The Hero with a Thousand Faces by Joseph Campbell
Quantum Questions: Mystical Writings of the World's Greatest Physicists Edited By Ken Wilber
Cosmos and Psyche by Richard Tarnas

Table of Contents

"Until a fact passes through your imagination, it's a lie." —
Stella Adler, *The Art of Acting*

Preface

There are two questions people often ask me upon hearing I am psychic. One is: Have you always known you are psychic? And my answer to this question is: No.

I awakened to my psychic mind around the age of thirty-four. It took a while to recognize it, but I came to notice too many coincidences between my thoughts and my subsequent reality for me to ignore. Over the course of about a year, a curious stream of serendipities led me to draw the conclusion that my mind had somehow turned psychic.

Of course it could also be said that I simply noticed something that was already there!

People commonly believe psychic ability is genetically wired into a few lucky (or unlucky) people. They believe "the gift", as it is so often called, can only be passed down from one generation to another. That's because most people who identify as psychic were taught, as children—usually by their mothers or grandmothers—that they could tap into the link between their imaginations and reality.

The rest of us are tacitly taught that the imaginary realm and the physical realm have no relationship to one another. But they are interwoven! Nothing comes to fruition without first being envisioned.

Psychic ability is a completely natural human function, available to anyone, at any time. Most of us haven't been taught to know or embrace it in ourselves. We've been taught to fear and deny it.

People have all manner of psychic experiences. Some people have visions of catastrophes that are extremely disconcerting for them. Some see things about their friends or family they would rather not know. Some become hosts to spirits they want nothing to do with. These have not been my experiences, and they don't have to be yours either.

Psychic insights are filtered through our emotions. Fear, anxiety, and other negative feelings will adversely influence psychic visions. I strive to approach the psychic mind with a sense of innocence, wonder, optimism and hope. When I am faced with a dilemma, and seeking insight through a psychic vision, I am asking myself, what would be wonderful, as an outcome?

We can't see the future as a whole. But we can see snapshots of it. Psychic visions are like simple, cleverly composed pictures presented in our imagination. Elements of the past and future are woven into them. They are usually symbolic in nature but sometimes they are literal.

We can create psychic visions, or they may come to us in our sleep. The conscious, thinking mind tends to place little value on them. But the creative, intuitive mind sees the symbols in these visions as rich with significance.

Witnessing a psychic vision play out in reality feels completely magical. Going about our business, an apparently unscripted event occurs; something we've previously dreamt or imagined. A canny aspect of our intelligence is partially unveiled, and we are left with a mystery. And maybe, even a clue to solving it.

I'm hoping this book will offer a practical reference point for your own psychic discovery. By observing how I experienced my psychic unfolding, perhaps you will see how your own psychic mind reveals itself to you. I believe that if you learn to cultivate, identify and follow psychic impressions, they will lead you—one coincidence at a time—on an exciting journey of transformation.

The other question people most often ask me upon hearing that I am psychic is: Can you turn it off?

When I first heard this question, I thought, turn off *what*? As I inquired into it, I came to understand that many people are under this misconception that psychics walk down the street with x-ray vision, seeing the past, present and future of every person passing by! Many people think psychics are walking portals with no control over their "visions." I'm hoping my book helps change this notion.

I've found my own journey of psychic awakening to be magical and empowering. It's enriched me as a creative being, added depth and perspective to my world-view, and helped me have a greater sense of possibility for myself. Maybe you'll have a similar experience.

Now when people ask me, Can you turn it off? I reply, Why would I want to do that?

Introduction

I was raised by a couple of bird watchers. Countless mornings in my youth were spent in the woods, by a lake, or at the ocean's edge in Rhode Island, observing birds with my father, mother and sister. Peering through binoculars, my father would say, "Is it a Veery?"

My mother, bird guide in hand, would retort. "No, Buzz. That's a Hermit Thrush."

"I don't think so, Fleurette. The chest! Look at the chest!" And a whispered debate would ensue until enough detail was observed about the bird to identify it.

This little facet of my life was brought to my attention upon my waking this morning– presented by my dream mind, my Spirit Guide, or the voice inside my head. Whatever you want to call it. My immediate question was why did my mind reflect this particular memory to me?

Then I realized that before going to sleep I'd asked myself, what in my history, accounts for my apparent psychic ability? I think this dream is my answer. I was brought up to investigate nature, and to notice details. My mother and father cultivated a sense of curiosity in me, and encouraged all their children in their creativity. I consider the qualities of curiosity, observation and creativity essential to my psychic awakening, and I am grateful to my parents for helping to instill them in me.

At eighteen, I was restless, and tired of the classroom. I skipped college, and took off to Hawaii. I got married and divorced, and finally, at twenty-six or so, accepted that I was gay and came out of the closet.

I enjoyed the sun, the ocean and the lau lau—a traditional Hawaiian dish of pork and fish wrapped in a taro leaf. And I made a lot of friends, especially by working in restaurants.

I started as a bus boy then moved up to assistant bartender, waiter, shift supervisor, and finally, manager. I wanted to create something, somehow make a difference in the world. But I felt like a cog in a machine. As I understood the corporate game, I'd get a nifty sounding title along with less pay and more work. In my search for something more rewarding, I decided to turn a hobby into a business. I had been making gourmet tropical ice creams and sorbets at home, so started my own ice cream company. For a few years, I enjoyed great success at it. But then things started going all wrong...

Meltdown

Hell Not

May 3, 2003

Afternoon

I'll start growing gills soon, it's so humid. Everything I touch sticks to me. I'd do anything for air conditioning, but there simply isn't enough money for it. Though two square window fans run at top speed above me, they provide little relief to my hot little ice cream plant.

"Hot little ice cream plant." I make it sound sexy, but believe me, it isn't. You've probably never had the pleasure of smelling a grease trap being emptied. It's something between a rotting carcass and a cesspool. And perhaps you've had a candy bar melt all over your fingers? That's cute. But if you had to mix, say, ten gallons of chocolate by hand, you'd have the stuff running down your legs.

In my business, viscous liquids, such as mango pulp, honey, and simple syrup, have to be extracted from ten gallon buckets and fifty five gallon barrels, then measured out according to various recipes. It's simply not possible to do this without getting some on the walls—no matter how careful you are.

If my plant were tiled like a shower stall, I'd just hose the whole thing down with hot water and bleach. But it isn't tiled like a shower stall. The walls are brick and craggy. And they've been covered over in places with a random patchwork of plywood and dry wall. There are more nooks and crannies around here than a Thomas' English muffin.

One of the previous tenants, a Chinese muu muu manufacturer, had, what has to be, miles of telephone and electric cables installed—none of it to code. It's all stapled to the walls. The next tenant, a pizza baker, just covered it all over with about nine coats of paint. Most of the recent coats have been white, but you can see green and orange underneath those in places.

My cement floor is full of cracks, and quite uneven. One area is painted a hunter green. The rest has been covered over with beige, household grade linoleum. Every time the floor is mopped, chips of paint and linoleum splatter onto the lower portion of the walls.

Amongst the payables I have on my desk is a worker's compensation insurance policy bill for $11,000. *$11,000!* All to insure my employees in case one of them should drop a bag of sugar on his foot. What a racket!

After entering the last of my banking transactions, I scroll down the window of my accounting program, and take a deep breath to prepare myself for the viewing of my business's checking account balance. Negative $3,326. Damn.

Over $5,000 in receivables is due to my company, but I'm not likely to see any of that before overdraft fees are incurred. I owe the bank several hundred thousand dollars. At the slim profit margins we're getting, I'd better sell a lot of ice cream—fast.

Everywhere I look I see the marks of a business hanging on to dear life. The stainless steel sink has a leg missing. It's propped up with a hunk of wood. My walk-in freezer is from the 1950's. It's patched up in places with duct tape.

A spigot protrudes out the freezer's side wall from a point about waist high. Every six hours the defrost cycle kicks in. Heating-coils melt the build-up of excess ice from within. The resulting water slowly drips from the spigot into an overflowing bucket beneath. In most commercial kitchens this water drips into a floor drain.

We don't have a floor drain.

With a sigh of depression I collect the water-bucket off the floor, bring it over to the sink (of course spilling some of it along the way) and empty it out.

Every once in a while, life presents us with a scene so bizarre and surreal that it is burned into our memory forever. Emptying the water bucket never fails to remind me of one such scene. One morning I came in to work to find three blind mice perched on this bucket's rim.

Not two mice, or four. But three, just like the nursery rhyme. And they really were blind! Having just been born, their eyes were still shut. How their mother deposited them there on the rim of this full bucket is still a mystery to me. The innate dexterity they had at that tender age amazed me. There they were, perched like birds on a wire, lapping away at the cool and refreshing water.

I was so freaked out at finding them, so appalled they were born in my kitchen that I couldn't dwell on my fascination for long. I had to kill them. After all, where was their mother? And how many other mice were there?

I carried out the gruesome task by tapping them into the bucket with a broomstick. It was traumatizing watching them thrash about and drown. I could hardly sleep for a week after that. Now I have to be reminded of this horrible little vignette every time my employees forget to empty the bucket.

How many times have I told them: *Don't forget to empty the water bucket!*

At the sink, I think of the money I spend keeping this place sterile, and the life of slavery that lies before me. To pay off my debt I'll be hand pouring ice cream, one cup at a time, until I die. I want to cry.

A Hawaiian Airlines jet screams by overhead. My walk-in freezer's motor wheezes and moans. At the warehouse next door, an eighteen wheeler issues a series of shrill beeps as it backs up to the loading dock. To cover all this up, I have the Village People cranked up really high. I'm gonna go deaf.

Listening to the Village People makes me think of Michael, my friend who also became my business partner. In the early days we would wait on tables at night, then come in and turn ice cream until three in the morning. We mainly serviced restaurants and hotels back then. The clients would call in the orders. We would fill them that night, and then deliver them the next day. We shared a lot of laughs as we built the company one client at a time. Finally, one day, we opened up a little retail store. It was our dream, come true.

One night, after one of my restaurant shifts, I walked into the production room to find Michael dancing to the Village People while a lemon sorbet turned in the ice cream machine. His apron was smeared with strawberry and chocolate, and he was singing into a spatula microphone.

"Young man, there's a place you can go.
I said, young man, when you're short on your dough.
You can stay there, and I'm sure you will find
Many ways to have a good time.

Bah! Bah! Bah! Bah! Y – M – C – A!"

"Michael! What if somebody saw you dancing like that through the windows!? This is *not* the neighborhood to be seen dancing to the Village People at two in the morning."

"Derek, they'll just have to get used to it. The Village People are in the hood!"

"Well, Kalani is sleeping right next door, Michael. You might want to keep it down."

"That janitor guy?"

"Yes. He's living there. With his girlfriend, and his dog. And maybe his daughter too."

"Derek, that guy's got a screw loose or something. He's really simple. I don't know how it is he runs that business. All he's ever said to me is, 'Ha ya doin' Michael?'"

"That's all he's ever said to me too!"

"That dog of his—I feel so bad for it. I think he neglects it."

"I know. It seems kind of sad or abused or something."

"Derek, what's that banging sound?"

I listen for the sound and say, "It's a truck backing in to the loading dock next door." As I say this, I realize I've been in a reverie. The sound of the truck is coming from reality. I'm not with Michael anymore. I'm alone.

About six months after our grand opening, Michael became gravely ill and suddenly died. Working this ice cream business hasn't been the same ever since. After struggling with it for about a year, I had to shut down the retail store.

Above me, an assortment of whisks, tongs, spatulas and spoons hangs from an improperly mounted ceiling rack. A couple of knives and a pastry bag lay on the stainless steel table. For a moment I imagine the place as an underground 1930's abortion clinic. God, how bizarre my mind can be! Why do I think things like that?

My imagination sure can be strange, but I love being in it. For a minute there, it really did seem like Michael was here. I can't see him now, but I can feel him. "Michael," I call out to the ether. "I can't do this business anymore, Michael!"

No response. "Michael! I found a dead black cat in front of our doorstep this week. You didn't send him to me, did you? As a sign or something?"

"Derek," Michael finally replies, "What do you take me for?"

In my mind's eye, he has returned. I see him standing on the butcher-block table. "Derek, we had our disagreements, but do you honestly think I would leave a dead black cat on your door step?"

"So you're telling me he just decided to die right there, in that particular spot, two feet in front of our front door?"

"Don't read too much into it."

"Michael, I'm reading into it! How can I *not* read into it? A black cat crosses your path, that's bad luck. Everyone knows that. But for a dead one to show up at your *front door*, that's... Well I don't know what that is, but it's not good."

"I'll send you a black cat alright—of another variety," he adds with a devilish smile. "He'll be *all* you can handle!"

"Michael, please."

"Derek, you need to let loose! Get your booty down!"

A tick is crawling up my arm, which, naturally, sends me into a state of confusion. What the hell is a tick doing here? In reality? Yes, reality! I am out of my reverie.

Damn! How the hell did a *tick* get on me? When was I walking through tall grass? I didn't know there were ticks in Hawaii. I pinch it between my fingers, making sure it's crushed to smithereens. Gross! All I do is kill things around here!

Walking to the bathroom to wash my hands, I pass through a hallway stacked with a vast arsenal of cleaning supplies: bleach, gloves, rodent traps, you name it. In the bathroom, a copy of a newspaper article on me and Michael hangs above the toilet. One of my employees has used a pen to draw eyelashes, pigtails and a dress on me. They love to make fun.

Posters of naked girls with open legs fill the rest of the space. Every time I wonder whether or not I should allow this, I come to the same conclusion— let it be. They're good guys. Two of them have been working for me for nearly four years. I'm grateful for their loyalty.

I'm done for the day. Here it is—a beautiful day in Hawaii—and I'm stressing out at work. All my friends are at the beach. I'm going to join them, damn it!

I head back to the production room, and over to the kitchen sink where I pour myself a glass of water from the tap. I have no qualms about drinking this water because I've had it tested in the lab. In fact, every month I get it tested and it comes out clean as a whistle every time. If there were bacteria *they* would find it too, like that time with the can opener...But I don't need to think about that.

As I stand at the sink, drinking my potable tap water, I stare out at a wall marked with chocolate stains. I used to like chocolate. I doubt I ever will now. Just as I am about to turn away, I see a small spot, moving across the wall. It's another tick! *What the hell?* I glance to the right and am stunned to find another one. And another. *Jesus!*

A creepy chill runs through me. Walking along the sink, I come to the wall adjoining Kalani's unit next door.

Several more brown spots are moving, ever so slowly, all at the same rate. I zoom in on one, then another. They're *all* ticks! Shifting my focus from floor to ceiling, I am horrified to discover that there are hundreds upon hundreds of them crawling all over the wall.

Acupuncture 101

May 28, 2003

Late Morning

Staring blankly at water-stained ceiling tiles, I take a deep breath and try to relax. I'm on a padded acupuncture table, shivering, either from the air conditioning or my fear—I can't tell which. My friend Will, who's been studying Taoist medicine, feels the souls of my feet then rubs his fingers together as if he were making the sign for money. "Mmm...Clammy," he remarks, making a note on his pad.

Will has been trying to get me on this table for weeks. He says acupuncture could be just the thing to cure me of a range of maladies—no doubt brought on by stress—which have recently afflicted me. He says the needles are small and that the treatment will be painless, but I'm not so sure.

Will is in his final year of schooling. It is not lost on me that I am probably his very first patient. I don't dare ask him about this. It's better if I remain ignorant. *Someone* has to be a brain surgeon's first patient. And how do you know that turbulent flight you're on isn't being flown by a pilot who's never been out of a simulated flight machine? You don't. And you don't ask either.

Will has provided the calming scent of lavender oil and the soft sounds of a Chinese flute to comfort me. But all I can think of is that in a few minutes I'm going to be stabbed with needles all over my body. I'm wondering if it's not too late to back out.

After I made this appointment a couple of days ago, I met two girls at a party who told me they pierced each other's ears at home, by hand, using only ice as a numbing agent. I thought, this is the Universe laughing at me—"See? *They* can do it."

I've read that creative visualization techniques can help in situations like this, so I spent all last night imagining this acupuncture session as a completely painless experience. In my vision, as Will stood over me, I turned to him and said, "Tell me when you're going to put the needles in." And he said, "I've put them in already. See? You didn't even feel it."

Last night this was easy to envision. But now that I'm actually on the table, my anxiety's back—I'm having a harder time seeing it.

"So the ticks were from your neighbor's dog?"

"Can you believe it? They said it was a nest! I shudder to think of what was on the other side of that wall! Ugh, the conditions that dog must have been living in. Not to mention Kalani, and his girlfriend. And maybe his daughter too. I mean, they're all *living* there. Naturally I called the landlord and made them fumigate. I want them evicted."

"Your nerves are shot, Derek." Will stands above me with a kind of shocked look on his face. He runs his eyes over my body, from my feet to my chest and back. I can tell he doesn't know where to begin.

Finally he asks, "What are your main complaints?" He seems determined to drag this out. I wish he would just put the needles in and get it over with. "Uh...my stomach and bowels give me trouble."

"The Chinese believe thoughts are digested as equally as food," he says.

We digest our *thoughts* as well as our *food*. I love that idea! I do tend to let my fears get the best of me. I walk through life with a vague anxiety that everything will tragically fall apart. I didn't used to be this way. But all this bad luck—starting with Michael's death about two years ago—losing the retail store, the dead cat, the mice, the ticks. It's all come to me in such dramatic fashion. Something's WRONG.

I'm not on the right path or something. My life isn't working. I have this sense that if I don't fix it some destructive event will come to correct things. And it won't be fun to go through. The department of health will shut me down...the bank will come in and repossess everything...I'll contract some dreadful disease.

Actually, the most obvious disaster would be for me to slip and fall on the water spilled from the mouse bucket. Yes, I'll slip and die of a concussion one Saturday morning. Then the power will go out, the freezer will defrost, and a pool of melted ice cream will flow out through the bottom of the door. Slowly, it'll wrap itself around me, and Sunday, as the plant gets hot, I'll bake in the cream. It'll be a holiday weekend. My employees will find me Tuesday morning covered with maggots.

"Headaches?"

"Huh? Oh." I shake my head, "No."

"That's a good sign." Thank God. He's ruling out something terminal.

I was going to be the Ice Cream Mogul, damn it! I was going to pave the world over with my ice cream outlets. Like Starbucks, there would be one on every third corner. I was going to start a foundation. Generations of children were going to idolize me. The whole dream used to be so easy to imagine. Now, I can't see it at all.

Will has moved over to his desk to type something into his laptop. "Will, don't you think passion fruit and banana sounds like a good flavor combination?"

"Hmm?"

"Banana and passion fruit. Doesn't that sound delicious? I call it Monkey Love! Isn't that clever? *I* think it's cute. But nobody buys that flavor. And it's good too! Haven't you tried it?"

"I don't know that I have."

"All they want is vanilla. The other day I'm in the supermarket aisle giving out samples. I offer Monkey Love to this old lady. She must've been about seventy-five years old, maybe even eighty. She sneers at me in disgust and says, 'I'm not gonna eat that!' Then she quickly jerks her hand up and down in the motion of a guy masturbating. She says, 'It reminds me of monkeys doing *this*!'

That's when I knew. I had to take it off the market."

Will chuckles at the computer. At least I think he does. He's reading up on something. Suddenly I become aware of myself splayed out on the table. It makes me feel vulnerable.

Yes, there's no doubt. Things will not be turning out as I had planned. I think we can safely say the evidence is in. I never thought of stress as contributing to my stomach trouble. I wonder if I have an ulcer.

Will asks, "How are you sleeping? Well?"

"I've been waking up in the night."

"What time?"

"Three. Four."

"Mmm. That's liver time."

"The liver has a time?"

"Yep."

"Does the pancreas?"

"Stick out your tongue."

"Aahhagh." Scrutinizing my mouth and throat, Will winces, and pulls back his head. No doubt there's a colony of killer bacteria living in there. "The tip of your tongue is red," he says. "Your heart is hot." My eyes become wide as I try to figure out what to make of this comment. Placing three fingers on my wrist, he says, "I'm feeling for your spleen pulse."

"I have a spleen pulse?"

"The spleen regulates digestion." As he says this, I hear a siren go off on the street below. Somehow, it seems perfectly timed, as if to serve as a warning sign.

"Your spleen pulse is barely detectable, Derek. You're having trouble digesting the new you." Will's language and methods are unusual to me, but he speaks so directly to my issues that I cannot question them. Lately, I've sensed that I'm in for some big changes in my life.

Will feels my other wrist. "You have no yin energy in your kidneys, Derek. You're not nurturing yourself."

Jesus, when are you going to learn to nurture yourself, Derek? How many times do you have to hear this from people? He adds, "You have plenty of yang energy there though. Entrepreneurs often have problems with kidney energy deficiency because they carry heavy burdens. Anxiety is the root cause of most kidney weakness."

Finally, he leans over the table, establishes clear eye contact with me, and says, "Four out of your five energy centers are shot. You need a routine healing modality like yoga or meditation, as well as ultra self emotional care."

His words have hit home. As I think about the crazy life I've created, Will rubs a cool alcohol swab over various points of my body. I feel like I'm spinning my wheels in my quest to get where I want to go in life. I've been living with financial uncertainty for as long as I can remember. Maybe I haven't really wanted to let go of the parts of my life that aren't working. Or known how. It seems I'd better figure out what I have to change—or else.

Turning my head away, I say, "Tell me when you're going to put the needles in."

"I've put one in already," he says. "See, you don't even feel it."

I can't help chuckling. That visualization technique really works! Will asks, "What's so funny?"

"Nothing."

He puts a needle into my foot. Ouch! Now that I'm paying attention, I notice the needles aren't totally painless. Funny, how the mind works.

With the last needle in, Will covers me with a blanket to keep me warm. I wonder if the blanket is bending the needles? He leaves me to lie out for a while. I thought it would feel painful with a bunch of needles in me, but I don't feel anything. Slowly I relax and actually become sleepy. I begin to wonder where my body is. I can't feel it the same way I usually do.

It's a trippy experience, and I find myself studying it, asking myself where my body is. Suddenly, I realize that I'm in a dream reality that allows me to see myself from a place deep inside myself. This is so unfamiliar that I can't describe it any other way. At my center there is a giant ball of light, which I see, but also know I am. I feel quite euphoric!

I become aware of a presence—a man. I can't see him, but only have a sense that he's around me. Sometimes I'm stopped at a traffic light, and feel someone is watching me. Often, I look over and sure enough, the person in the next car has been looking at me. This is how I sense the man.

The man says, "You are learning the science of mind. Your imagination is a powerful and magnificent tool. Use it to create any reality you wish."

The ball of light has become a white cloud, which I am within. I emerge from it, and see myself standing on a stage, like an orchestra conductor. A large group of people sits in front of me, all with their eyes closed. They're in lotus position, levitating about three feet off the floor.

Another voice, from somewhere beyond this plane, softly calls to me. "Okay, Derek. I'm going to take the needles out now."

Fire and Ice

June 12, 2003

Afternoon

I have been home now for two days, in a funk, avoiding work. Overwhelmed by a life I've created that is no longer working for me, I seek direction by flipping some tarot cards. Every day I ask the same questions: "Who am I? What can I do with my life? Most of all, How can I turn my ice cream company into a success?"

A few years ago my company was listed in one of the local business newspapers as the 17th Fastest growing business in Hawaii. The mayor gave me an award for hiring from the city's Welfare to Work program—A Most Outstanding Employer. Our clients included Japan Airlines and Neiman Marcus. The market is small here in Hawaii, that's all. You can't start this kind of enterprise on a dime. You need millions, that's all there is to it. I feel like I'm on the Titanic. The ship is going down, and I'd better get on a life raft— fast.

When I think of the slim profit margin I'm netting, I picture myself hand-pouring ice cream cups for the next twenty years. 10,971...10,972...10,973...No way!

I flip three tarot cards from Aleister Crowley's Thoth deck. Help me!

I get the High Priestess, Eight of Disks, and Art. For a while, I just stare at them having no clue as to what they could mean. I look through some tarot books for the meaning of the cards. They describe the High Priestess as a card of intuition, the

Eight of Disks as a card of apprenticeship, and Art as a card of healing.

I can't see how this will help me at all. Intuition. What the hell am I supposed to do with that? It's so vague. And how's the Art card supposed to save me?

I look over that card again. It shows a picture of a woman mixing fire and ice together in a cup. Fire and ice don't go together. I don't get it.

Looking into the card, I ask, "What do you have to say to me, Lady?"

"I am ice, and I burn," she replies.

Yeah, that makes a lot of sense.

Out of a need to entertain myself, I decide to work on a stenciling project I've had in mind. I've wanted to paint a wavy line, with some silver stars laid over it along the upper perimeter of my living room walls. Over the last couple of days I've gathered some tools together to complete the job; tracing paper, some cardboard, a razor blade, pencils, a few plastic cut outs of stars. I turn on some Bonnie Raitt, and begin working.

Half an hour later, my friend Mike calls, from Maui. "Come on, Sister," he says. "You need a break. Why don't you fly over for the weekend?"

I take him up on his offer. Thank God for friends!

The Stars, Waving

June 14, 2003

Early Evening
"I sold Tom this unit," Mike says, as we approach his friend Tom's front door. Maui's real estate is booming and Mike has been making a fortune. Why can't I hit my stride like him? "I'm going to buy unit 401 down the hall," he continues, "but Tom's got the best condo in the building. It's an end unit with high ceilings and a clear view of the ocean." Tom greets us, offers us a drink and immediately takes us on the grand tour of his new place. He excitedly shares all his interior decorating plans with us.

"...and along here," Tom says, pointing to the upper edge of a hallway wall, "I'm going to paint a wavy line with some stars laid over it."

Hell, Yes

June 18, 2003

Morning

It's with a raging hangover that I pull up to the ice cream plant. Why did I go out last night?

9am, and it's already sweltering outside. Someone left a couple of trash bags out by the curb. An animal or vagrant must have ripped them open in the night because garbage is strewn all over the sidewalk. It's going to be one of those days, I can tell.

I've got a meeting with a vendor at ten, then deliveries to make, ice cream to turn, and inventory to record. Today's our fumigation day. We'll have to wrap up production by four o'clock.

I don't see any of my employees' cars. I hope someone gets here soon. I'm going to need another coffee. Definitely. More coffee.

Stepping up to the door, I smell smoke—the chemical kind. Damn! What the hell is this?

The plant's been broken into three times since I've been here. For added security, I've had three locks put on the doors. Frantically, I get them all unlocked. Inside, I'm greeted by hissing and crackling sounds. I deduce that the fire is electrical. My office is filled with smoke.

Stepping around the corner, I find my walk-in freezer completely buckled in on itself, melted to the ground. About fifty gallons of ice cream is oozing like lava across the floor of the plant.

Damn it!

Psychic Guidance

July 1, 2003

Afternoon

Sitting on my parked motorcycle, I stare like a zombie at a flattened drinking straw lying in a patch of crabgrass at the side of the road. I'm not even sure what I'm doing here. When you can't come up with your own answers, I guess you start stabbing in the dark. For whatever reason, I expressed interest in seeing a psychic to two separate people and each one of them happened to recommend the same guy. I took it as a sign to see him.

I've never seen a psychic before. Should I ask questions? Or just listen? He specializes in astrology apparently. And he's a channel too. I'm not sure what that's about. I'll bet I'm a case study though. I must look like I've been walking circles in the desert for weeks. I can imagine him looking at my chart and having to call a colleague for advice.

When did I get this cynical? I never used to be so self-deprecating.

Arnold's house is high up on the mountain of Wilhelmina Rise, tucked into a buckle of land in such a way that prohibits it from getting much light. What a pity to be all the way up here and not get a view of the ocean, or even the city. He's got a nice mango tree in his yard though.

Nobody's home, but I'm early. Hopefully he'll show up. For the third time, I check a piece of paper in my pocket to make sure I have the right address. Yeah, this is the place.

An old, white Ford LTD pulls up. A man, presumably Arnold, gets out carrying a take-out order of Chinese food. I get the impression he'd rather eat his lunch than see me. He looks my way, but doesn't greet me. "I'll just put this in the fridge," he says, climbing the stairs to the front door. No proper greeting. Something feels wrong, but I follow him inside anyway.

The smell of incense, essential oils, and Indian spices greet me as I enter the house. A woman, who looks like she had a lot of fun in the seventies, chants quietly in a small room to the left of the doorway. She sits in a semi-lotus position, rocking back and forth, shaking a rattle. When I first arrived at the house I rang the doorbell about five times. I must have disturbed her.

Arnold takes me into a room to the right, points to a well worn sofa, then leaves, saying he has to print out my astrological chart. His couch sucks me in a little too deeply for my taste. I imagine it alive, eager to swallow me for lunch. What the hell am I doing here? This place is like a little shop of psychic horrors.

I catch myself gripping the armrest too tightly. I take a breath and relax, folding my fingers together over my lap. At my feet, a thick layer of dog hair covers an old Indian carpet. A black candle burns on a shelf above me like The Eye of Providence. Next to that, an impatient clock taps its fingers on the wall.

There might be some wisdom in this psychic reading. Probably some junk though too. I hope I can sort through it.

Arnold walks in with my astrological chart and sits in a leather chair opposite me. After glancing at it he says, "You have an uncle who passed away? Uh...maybe ten years ago?"

"Yes."

"He had business skill and humor."

"Yes, he did, both. That would be him." *How does he know this?*

"He is here with other members of your family who've passed. And there are some personal guides also. They've formed a kind of counsel to look after you, as it seems you're going through a difficult time."

"I have an ice cream business that's pretty severely in debt. Things keep going wrong. It's been causing me stress."

"Your uncle seems to speak to this issue. Do you know why?"

"Yeah, I guess it makes sense. Having a business is stressful. He owned a funeral home. He supported a wife and six kids with it, which I always found amazing. He died a little young, at sixty-nine. I think it all caught up with him."

"They're giving me a message for you. The message is that if you don't release yourself from this ice cream business, you're going to get sick. And not a little sick either. This one would be a doozie."

As I receive this information, fear and dread races through me. I'm holding on to the word "if". It's not too late to avoid disaster. "Your guides also recommend that you look for obvious signs, coincidences, that sort of thing. They want you to know that these signs mean they're helping you. When you ask for help from your guides, they'll provide it. But you have to ask for help. Otherwise it won't come."

We each sit for a moment in silence. Is it my imagination? Or am I slipping deeper into the sofa? "I have a question," I say.

"What is it?"

"If I leave this business, I'm not really sure what I can do. I love acting, and I've been reading tarot cards, but I don't think I can make a living out of either."

"You will always work for yourself. I can see that," he replies. Thank God. I never want to work for anyone else ever again.

Looking off to the side, he squints his eyes and adds, "You're going to use the computer as the centerpiece of your business. You have natural psychic ability. You can use it to counsel others. The acting will follow from that." Chuckling, he adds, "You will play a very interesting character later on in life."

For nearly an hour Arnold relays insights like this to me. Suddenly, in the middle of a sentence, he raises a finger up and cocks his head, as if he heard a strange sound in the next room. With great urgency he says, "One of my spirit guides wants to talk with you, directly. I'll be tuning out for a few minutes, letting him speak through my body, okay?"

"Okay." I guess...

Arnold drops his jaw to his chest, and for a minute, it appears as if he is falling asleep. His chair also seems to be sucking him in.

"I am a member of the afore-mentioned council," Arnold says, except the voice I hear is not his. It's deeper, more British in tone. Arnold's body has gone totally limp. He's like a puppet.

"I'd like to remind you of an incantation you wrote in another lifetime, some two hundred years ago, earth time. We think it would serve you well now." What a strange and quirky entity this guy is! He's pretty old if he's been around for two hundred years. And he says "we" as if he speaks on behalf of the whole group.

An image comes to me, in which I was a kind of psychological pharmacist. I picture myself in a quaint house nestled deep in the forest. A warm fire burns in the corner of the room. People drop in from miles around, seeking my spiritual remedies. I write some thoughts, which might be described as mental prescriptions, on small scrolls. I have my patients tuck them in their pockets or under their pillows. "Say this once in the morning and twice at night," I tell them, with an encouraging wink and a reassuring smile. "There's magic in these words. The *words* are *magic*!"

"Nothing in this world," the voice speaking through Arnold dramatically intones, "can withstand my will."

I listen intently.

"For the power divine

Is governing still
I am one with that light
I am one with that power
And it makes me more joyous
And magical each hour

The future before me
Is an open book
I see where my path lies
With just one look
And so all things
I need are here
My life proceeds
In directions clear

So be it
So be it
So be it"

A cloud must have blocked the sun, for the room is suddenly quite dark. A swift breeze rings three bars of a chime hanging outside the window.

The woman who was chanting in the other room enters with the phone in her hand. "Arnold, your next client."

I scramble awkwardly out of the seat. "Let me pay you," I say, pulling out my wallet. "One hundred and twenty five dollars, I believe your secretary said." Arnold pauses for a moment, after taking the phone, then says, "You can just leave me a hundred."

Ask Your Angels

July 2, 2003

Afternoon

"Do you want me to call you back? I can pay for this call." It's my mother, in Rhode Island.

"No, Mom, it's fine. I can pay for it. I can't talk long anyway. I just wanted to tell you about my session with the psychic."

"Oh?"

"I loved it! It was amazing. As soon as I walked out of there, I thought to myself, I want to do what he does."

"Well this is certainly the happiest I've heard you in a while."

"I feel like he gave me clarity. He even sensed my financial situation and gave me a break on the price. And Uncle Tom was there."

"Really?"

"He picked right up on him. It struck me as strange because I wasn't really that close to Uncle Tom. I wondered, Why him? The only thing I could come up with is that Uncle Tom was an undertaker; he buried the dead. Maybe he's trying to tell me I need to bury my business."

"Uh huh."

"Mmm, I guess that's a stretch. I don't know. But he said Uncle Tom was part of a council of spirit advisors and suggested I look for obvious signs that they were helping me. And I think I'm already seeing them. This morning, I was walking by this weird little mystical shop and something told me to go in. There was a woman in there doing psychic readings. She had crystals and incense— "

"You didn't pay for another reading, did you?"

"No, Mom, I didn't."

"Good, because you need to spend your money wisely."

Eye roll. "Yes, Mother. As I was saying, she sells new age stuff, and off to the side, there was a shelf with used books on it. One was titled, *Ask Your Angels* and it was only $5.00. You know, I just knew it was for me. I knew it. I've been meditating, trying to reach the head of the council."

"Well, you know your father has benefitted greatly from meditation."

"I know he has. One of my friends gave me a book on self hypnosis, so I want to see what I can do with that."

"How are things at work?"

"Dreadful. My walk-in freezer burnt down."

"You're kidding!"

"Right to the floor."

"How can a freezer catch on fire?"

"The defrost cycle got stuck in the on mode. The wires were frayed." As I say these words, something niggles at me. "Oh my God, Mom! I drew a tarot card a while ago, and it had a woman on it mixing fire and ice. She said, 'I am ice and I burn.' I didn't get it at the time. But now I think she was referring to this incident with my freezer."

Broadcast

August 23, 2003

Mid Afternoon

I live on the top of a mountain, in a neighborhood of Honolulu called Alewa Heights. From my futon chair in my living room, I gaze out at shifting ripples of silvery light reflecting off the Pacific Ocean. Outside my front door I have a huge lanai full of happy plants, and a small table with two chairs. There's a fragrant Plumeria tree, a fruitful guava tree behind my mailbox, and an orange blossom bush along the side of the driveway. A tall macadamia tree at the edge of my neighbor's property constantly chatters in the wind.

I feel like a king in my house on the mountain! Except that I'm *renting* the place. I have never felt so poor and so rich at the same time. I hope I can continue to afford to stay here.

I'm in somewhat of a trance, having just come out of a self-guided meditation. I can't say I felt any particular peace or anything. Mainly, all I experienced was the talk of my conscious mind. There were pockets of silence, I suppose.

I've been meditating in order to contact my spirit guide. I haven't felt much success. Every book I read says I have to keep practicing, no matter what I feel.

I let out a sigh, and gaze out at the horizon. A memory flashes to mind, in which I was in outer space. It's so clear to me that I can't believe I forgot it. For a moment I wonder if it's something I just now imagined. But I'm sure it's from the meditation. Perhaps I was asleep instead of meditating, and didn't realize it.

I was floating between a pair of gigantic loudspeakers, each taller than a skyscraper. An unseen man stood at an unseen microphone. I could hear his breathing, and even see the woofers vibrate from the sound of his breath. I was to be on the alert for an important word that was about to come out of the two huge woofers. The man in the universe was about to speak. Time slowed, and with great anticipation I waited for the word. Finally, it came—fat, deep, and clear: "*BROADCAST*!"

What a strange little dream! Why does my mind conjure things like this? I can't see how any of it is significant, or what I'm to do with it. Is someone trying to broadcast to me? Am I to broadcast something? Maybe it means the Universe is broadcasting to me.

Searching for some meaning, I look up the word broadcast in my dictionary. In a new meditation journal I've been keeping, I write, "transmit by radio and television."

Registering The Signs

Portland Schmortland

September 3, 2003

Late Morning
Not all my friends know I've been into this new age stuff. I'm sure they would be fine with it, but I don't want anyone thinking I've gone wacko. My friend Michelle, however, is really into it. I've given her a couple of tarot card readings and she insists I have psychic talent. She talked to her friend Uma about me, and immediately Uma wanted a reading.

When Uma called me, she asked how much I charge. I exclaimed, "Oh, I don't do this for a living! I couldn't possibly charge you anything."

"But Michelle says you're really good," she said. "Can't I leave you a donation?" And that's how I got roped into this reading. Now Uma's at my house, sitting across from me, eagerly anticipating precious psychic information. And the only thing I can think is, *I don't know a thing about her!*

I wonder how much money she's going to leave me. Maybe twenty dollars? Twenty dollars to me is like a hundred dollars to most of my friends. I'd be happy with it. Maybe she'll leave fifty!

Her nervous energy doesn't help my anxiety. I'll bet she's afraid of what I'm going to say. As she waits for me to talk, she nonchalantly casts her gaze over to an Indonesian mask I have hanging on the wall. She rather obsessively combs her fingers through her long, straight hair, as if it might become tangled at any moment.

I close my eyes, but all I see is black. I'm trying my hand at this psychic technique I read about where you peer into the subtle shapes that form behind your eyelids when you close your eyes. She's waiting for me to say something profound. If I am silent any longer she will assume I am lost. Which I am!

A voice in my head says, "Fake it 'til you make it, Derek." *There's* some brilliant wisdom. I ask, "Do you sew?"

"No."

"Hmmm. It's just that in my mind's eye, I distinctly see a pin cushion." Actually, I only *vaguely* see a pin cushion. To be honest, what I saw looked more like a voodoo doll; pins, all stuck in a human shaped figure, but the image wasn't very defined at all.

I must appear confident. That much I understand. All the guide books say the same thing— Trust what you see. "You don't have any tailoring projects coming up, anything like that?"

"No. Not that I can think of."

Damn. I'm *wrong*. I ask for a psychic vision and *this* is what I get? A *voodoo doll?* Scary. For lack of anything else to say, I say, "Should you get pricked by a pin or have to do some tailoring, it's a sign to pay attention. There's something meaningful in it for you."

"Okay," she says.

What a goon I am! What the hell is *that* little piece of advice supposed to mean?

"I'm planning a trip," she says, changing the subject.

"And..."

"Can you tell me about it?"

How am *I* supposed to know where you're going? Psychic Gods, *please* help me see where she is going. I close my eyes, but all I see is the shape of a coffee cup. A *coffee cup?* What the *hell* am I supposed to do with that?

Coffee...A place famous for good coffee...Seattle? Seattle is famous for its coffee houses. Behind my eyelids, I see the shape of an arrow, pointing down. Not Seattle. "Some place south of Seattle, is what I see. Like Portland," I tell her.

"You mean California?"

Be confident Derek! What do you have to lose? "No, this place is famous for coffee. I can say that at least. I don't think it's California. I'm pretty sure I would've seen an avocado or something if it was California."

What the hell kind of conversation is this? Avocados. Coffee. "I see you in a Northwestern city, like Portland," I say, with as much confidence as I can.

"I've never been to Portland. And I hate the cold. I would never go there," she replies, dismissing the notion.

"Then I don't know what to tell you." Jesus, this is going great.

I glance down at a tarot card; the eight of pentacles. A student is pictured, writing in a book. Something about the student's eyes remind me of Uma's eyes, so I let the student represent Uma. "I see you as a writer," I say. Uma's face lights up like a Christmas tree.

Finally! I've hit upon something. From the expression on her face I can see she is excited by this notion. "Yes, you're going to write a book," I say with feigned confidence. "An idea you have for it seems to come from a dream." I don't know why I add this.

I look to the side for a moment. In my imaging faculty, the pages of a book are flipping. I have the sense that words are on them. "Wait," I add. "The book is already somewhat conceptualized, even written to some degree, no?"

"I've been keeping a journal."

"I see that. Stick with it. You're going to compile that into something big. It's going to be very well received." I just want to encourage her. She's so excited about it. Besides, in my imagination, there *are* words on the page.

Hmm. A journal is like a diary. "The story you want to write will come from your daily activities and experiences?"

Uma smiles. "Yeah."

I'd love to do that. "You have a gift for observing details, Uma. I imagine it's the story of a woman and her place in the world. But you're too preoccupied to write it right now." You're guessing, Derek. What the hell. I'm probably right. "Your time is being sucked up by something else. Is this school?"

"Uh huh."

"It feels high level." I have no idea why I say this. I don't know what I'm talking about.

"I'm getting my PhD. Am I going to finish?"

Oh. I guess I was right. And no wonder the cards show her as a student, writing. You've got to write a thesis to get a PhD. This girl's smart.

I don't feel good all of a sudden. I can't explain it. But this feeling causes me to say, "You hate it, don't you?" Uma sighs deeply in frustration. I've nailed it.

I'm feeling empowered to continue with my train of thought. "You're wondering *how* you're going to finish your thesis, not *IF*. And probably, most importantly, *why*? It's not related to what you ultimately want to do, isn't it? You've lost interest." Uma nods. "But you've been going at it for so long and you're so close to the finish line? You saw this PhD as your ticket to fulfillment, and now you're questioning it."

Uma nods in agreement. A tarot card picturing a scowling old man catches my eye. I hold the card up to her. "See this old guy? Seems kind of determined to me."

"My grandmother."

"Oh. She's a tough customer?" Uma smiles and then starts crying. Oh, my goodness. She's really affected by this. "You're doing it to please her, aren't you?" She nods. "You have to please yourself as far as your work goes, Uma. Be happy doing what you do."

Ever so briefly, ever so faintly, a red curtain flashes in my mind. It reminds me of a theatre curtain. "Do you have an interest in theatre, Uma?"

Uma bursts out in tears and smiles. I've touched on something big. "Oh my God," she cries. "There's this guy, Jerry, who I want to work with at this theatre..."

I don't feel good again. "Well, I think Jerry might not be your guy as far as helping you in that regard."

"Shit. I knew it."

"He doesn't have the follow-through or something."

Exasperatedly, she says, "I know." This is amazing. I'm gathering this information from my feelings.

"But you're going to be supported in this, Uma. You're going to be given opportunities to make this happen, so don't get discouraged." I just want to support her at this point, say some encouraging words. "I see a successful book for you, or a play. The book was shown to me. When you write, give yourself a structure or framework and work within that. It's like writing a poem and choosing to do it in iambic pentameter or something. OK?" *Derek, where are you getting this stuff?*

"Yeah. Okay. I get it. Thank you."

After spending an hour with Uma, I end the reading. She thanks me again and leaves an envelope on my kitchen table.

Outside, I stand near my mailbox and wave to her as she drives off. As soon as she rounds the bend I run into the house and open the envelope. I feel like a kid opening a Christmas card from Grandma!

The envelope contains a card with a fifty-dollar bill in it. *Fifty dollars!* On the card, Uma wrote—presumably before the reading, for she never had time to do it afterwards—"Thank you for sharing your gift."

The sentiment is too much for me. Tears pour out of my eyes. "Oh God!" I blow out some candles I'd lit for Uma's reading, then pick up my phone and call my friend Michelle. "Hey, it's me," I say, when she answers. "I just finished with Uma."

"How did it go?"

"I have no idea. She left me fifty dollars though."

"That's great!"

"I'm not sure I earned it, Michelle. Some of the stuff was...well, sometimes I felt connected with her and at other times I didn't."

"Isn't that the way it goes though?"

"I guess. I don't know. I honestly don't know if I can do this, Michelle. It's like I'm selling air."

"Well I talked with her and she loved it."

"What do you mean, you talked with her? She just left!"

"I know. I was on the phone with her when you called."

"Oh my God. I can't believe she called you that fast. What did she say?"

"Well, we didn't have long to talk!" Michelle laughs. "She said she loved it. You were spot on. She says she has a new direction. She seemed excited about it."

"God, it's just that some of my perceptions seemed so off, that's all."

"But that's to be expected. I'm telling you Derek, you're good."

"Well, I gotta figure out how to get clients now. It's one thing reading for you and some friends, but I've got to figure out how to reach more people."

"They'll come. You'll see."

"God, Michelle, fifty dollars, and I don't have to pay any worker's compensation insurance out of it. If I can do this..."

"You can."

"But I don't trust I can see the right things for people. Like lately I keep seeing signs of the devil everywhere. And I don't understand what it means. I can't be talking with people about that!"

"What do you mean?"

"Well, my friend invited me to this cocktail fundraiser. One of the appetizers served was deviled eggs. The next morning I'm vacuuming my carpet, and I notice the brand name of my vacuum cleaner is Dirt Devil. My friend Steven calls me and as he's telling me a story, he says, "The devil is in the details." Then—get this, because here's the kicker—I went to the health food store, to the hot food bar. You pay by weight there, right? I get to the cash register, and the bill comes out to $6.66."

"Oh my God! All that *happened*?"

"Yes! Now wouldn't you suspect there was a *message* in all this if it happened to you? It's so freaky."

"You have to write about this, Derek. You have so many great stories. Things just happen to you. Like all your business stories. Remember when you moved into that space you were going to convert into a retail store, and your foot fell through the floor?"

"Michelle, the last thing I want to do is tell stories about my ice cream business. Please."

"Well, your life is so exciting compared to other people. This stuff can't be happening for nothing." □

"I don't see what's so great about it. I have no money...I'm *lost...I...*"

"Derek, you make life happen. That's what you do. And I've never seen anyone do it like you. When you want something, you don't just dream about it, you *do* it. How many other people would have started an ice cream company? Most people only dream about working for themselves. But you *did* it."

"Well, thanks for the encouragement, but I can't feel so great right now. I'll figure it out, I know I will. It just hurts is all."

For about a minute, we each keep silent. But I know Michelle is still on the line. One of the things I love about talking on the phone with Michelle is that we can sit for long stretches of time in silent contemplation.

Finally I say, "I looked up the devil card in one of my tarot books. It suggested a need to laugh, that I'm taking things too seriously. It also said I might be in a catch-22 type of situation. I'm shackled to this business, Michelle. I don't have any good options for leaving. I mean, I'm fighting some pretty impossible odds here. Ice cream is a commodity. The major brands we compete with are produced on the mainland, cheaply. They have the advantage because of cost efficiencies they get through volume and...Oh, I'm whining."

"You're not whining."

"I never thought I would want to leave my company. I never thought of failure. The best option I have right now is bankruptcy. Have you ever seen a picture of the devil card in the tarot? It's of people shackled in chains. They say it comes up when you feel like you're being controlled. Well, the debt's controlling me. I could get out of debt, but it would mean that I work for slave wages for the next twenty years. I can't do it. My body can't do it."

"You'll figure it out. Bankruptcy doesn't have to be so bad."

"Maybe."

"Okay. I gotta go."

"Michelle?"

"Mmm?"

"Thanks. I really appreciate it."

Stars From Mars

November 14, 2003

Afternoon

For a moment I'm not quite sure where I am. My eyes are closed, and I don't want to open them. I vaguely remember being in the woods, but I can feel now that I'm in my meditation chair. My hands were resting on my lap, but I can't feel them anymore. "They are no longer your hands anyway," a voice in my head says.

No longer my hands? How much time has past? I liked the woods. I want to go back.

In my mind, I am a huge tree. I don't see myself. But I know myself as sap, cells and bark. Through my roots, I drink water, from deep within the earth, with a quiet, deliberate focus.

A white flower with a yellow center twirls slowly before me. I am drawn to its stamen, which is coated with a glistening fluid...so mesmerizing! It's a portal of some kind.

It *is* a portal, isn't it? Let me find out.

Colors streak past me like I'm going at high speed. I feel like I'm on an amusement park ride. Suddenly, the colors are gone and I find myself standing in a dry, barren landscape sprinkled with small, red rocks.

Mars.

It's nighttime and the atmosphere is wonderfully silent. The sky is black, sprinkled with myriad stars. A middle-aged man with a stoic demeanor, wearing khaki pants and a collared shirt, approaches me from several yards away.

"You create the severity level of your own lessons," he says sternly, as he nears me.

"Hello to you too," I convey back to him, indignantly. Our thoughts are telepathic. There is no need to say anything aloud.

He seems to want to prove a point. I know he knows I'm curious about his attitude toward me, but instead of explaining it to me, he impatiently asks, "Are you listening?"

Something is familiar about this guy. We have a history. I'm trying to figure out what it is. He's not my brother from a past life, but... I quietly stand, giving him my attention.

"Are you *listening*?" he repeats, obviously irritated with me. His tone makes me think of my father scolding me when I was a teenager. I remember my father raising his voice to me, saying, "You *hear*, but you don't *listen*!"

The guy in khakis says, "I want to show you something."

I roll my eyes. "Jesus, if you want to *show* me something, why have you been making such a point that I have to *listen* to you?"

"Do you remember when you were asking me about how to develop your psychic ability and I suggested you feel with your taste buds and see with your ears?"

"Uh..." I remember writing *something* about that in my dream journal. But I forget it now. And anyway, it sounded irrelevant.

"I'm trying to get you to stretch," he says.

"Okay, already! You want me to think outside of my box. I get it."

We stand there a moment. I have my eyes cast down to the ground. He just stares at me. He's wearing loafers, and I notice his khaki pants are cut to a perfect length. He's dressed so conservatively that I wonder aloud, "If you're my spirit guide, shouldn't you be wearing robes or something?"

"Pick up a rock and throw it as far as you can."

"Okay. Fine. This is not a two way conversation." I pick up a rock and throw it for him. In the dark, it's hard to see where it lands but we hear it fall about twenty yards away. He stands there for a moment, shaking his head in disappointment; a gesture that says, what am I going to do with you?

He picks up a similar rock and throws it as high and as far as he can. His rock travels well above the horizon, deep into the atmosphere, where it ignites, and forms an arc, as a beautiful, silent, shooting star.

Interpreting the Language of Symbols

November 15, 2003

Morning

After reviewing my journal entry from yesterday, I wonder about some of the symbolism in it. The details in my meditative journeys must matter in some way that I am not currently aware. Otherwise, why would they be there? For example, what's up with that guy's conservative attire? Why was he so stern with me? Who *was* he? And why were we on Mars?

Stars played a part in that psychic vision of Tom's stencil motif on Maui. Now here they are again. Maybe the stars are trying to tell me something.

I've collected a bunch of books on interpreting symbols and dreams. I flip through some of them, in search of the word *clothes*. I doubt it will be listed.

I'm wrong. I guess everything is a symbol. Even clothes. Clothes seem to represent our outer persona, how we present ourselves. They define the characters we play in life.

I can't stand khaki pants. They're too conservative for me. I don't own a pair, and I hope I never do. Mostly, I like to wear jeans. So why would my spirit guide (if that is who he is) be wearing them? Is he suggesting I dress better?

I remember reading somewhere that every person who appears in one's dreams represents an aspect of one's self. I wonder if the impatient nature of the guy in my journey was a reflection of how hard I've been on myself lately? The chimes on my lanai ring in the wind, and I have the distinct feeling they're affirming this thought. I make a mental note to listen out for when they ring. Maybe they're a kind of oracle.

I look up the word Mars. Mars is about asserting one's power, especially toward the goal of bringing about prosperity. This message certainly seems relevant.

The shooting star seems, to me, to be a symbol of luck and good wishes. To see a shooting star is a fortunate experience, the result of having cast one's gaze in the right direction, at the right time. And stars from Hollywood are famous! Perhaps I'm in for a little fame!

I could've thrown the rock as far and high as the guy did. All I had to do was imagine it. It seems he's telling me not to limit myself.

In my imagination, I return to that place on Mars where the guy and I met. He appears, and says, "The laws of physics don't apply in the psychic realm. Reach for the stars, my friend."

Mars Landing

November 30, 2003

Late Morning

The B-52 cockroach air raid is an annual event up here on Alewa Drive. Roaches appear to multiply more rapidly during the rainy season. One night, every year, they come in droves—hundreds of them—clicking and clacking, dive bombing into the screens of my windows. Perhaps they're attracted to the lights in the house. For whatever reason, they appear desperate to get in.

The first year, they crawled in five, six at a time, scampering across the floor. I felt like I was in a horror flick. Last night, they were out on my lanai in full force. I had to stuff towels under the doors.

What is it with me and bugs lately? There is no denying, I've been having too many weird encounters with them. One message seems clear enough: *something's bugging me.*

Everything has been going wrong. It's like I've been attracting problems. A voice within me, that I'm guessing is my conscience, says, *Perhaps it's your pessimistic attitude.*

I don't see how I can grow my ice cream company anymore. I created it, but my job is done there. Now I wonder where my passion's gone. The type of work the company requires of me is not what I want to do. All these troubles I've been having—*they're signs.*

It's with great caution, that I approach my mailbox because I know there are about a dozen giant roaches lurking in the back corners of it. *Ugh*! I get the shivers just thinking about it.

Who knew roaches loved envelop glue? If I let a couple of days go by without pulling the mail out, they'll eat through the glue and open everything.

In one swift motion, I open the box. Sure enough, three huge monsters scurry to the back. Quickly, I pull the mail out as if it were on fire and would burn me. I let it all fall to the ground. A cockroach comes out with the mail and runs in circles around my feet. I end up doing a little dance to avoid him. *Hope the neighbors aren't watching.*

Amongst the mail is a familiar large, brown envelop. This month's National Geographic! Thanks Mom! The other three pieces are junk.

I rip open the magazine wrapper and sit down at the table on my lanai. The picture on the cover sends a chill through my body. It's the planet Mars.

I flip through the issue for a while, but I'm too distracted by the coincidence of seeing the planet show up in this way to really take in any of it. After about ten minutes, it strikes me that I should be more productive with my day.

On the way to the kitchen to wash my breakfast dishes, I notice the light on my answering machine, blinking. That's strange. I don't remember a call coming through. I press play and hear my friend Larry thanking me for the time we spent together the other night. Larry's a gem! We share everything with each other and can talk for hours about lovers, friends, dreams...all of life.

In his message to me, he uses the oddest choice of words! I have to press the playback button again, just to make sure I heard him right. "Hey Derek, I got a lot out of our talk last night. I really appreciate you broadcasting your ideas to me like that..."

Broadcasting my ideas? What the hell does he mean by that? I wonder what made him choose that word. It was just the two of us at dinner. It wasn't like I was yelling or anything when I talked with him.

The phone rings, interrupting my thought. "Hello?"

"Hi Derek, it's Nazarene." Nazarene is my talent agent. When she finds a role on a commercial project that I might be suited for, she calls me.

"Hi Nazarene!"

"You auditioned for the Central Pacific Bank commercial last week?"

"Yes, I did."

"You've been cast."

"Wow! Terrific!"

"They're wondering if you're available for filming this Wednesday."

"Yes! I can be free."

"Someone will call you with the exact call-time and location."

"Okay."

"Now for wardrobe, they're looking for a conservative look. Do you have a pair of khaki pants and a collared shirt?"

A tingling runs through me. "Uh...Yes," I lie.

"Good. Wear what you have, and bring a few extra shirts, if you have them."

Follow Me!

December 12, 2003

Early Afternoon

Since my company seems to be going to hell in a hand basket, I've decided to take the day off from work. It doesn't seem to matter if I show up or not. I figure I might as well go to the beach.

As I get on my motorcycle, I wonder about all the coincidences I've been having. They must be attempting to communicate something.

What function do signs serve? Are these the signs that Arnold talked about; the ones that are supposed to come from my council of angels? And if the signs are from the council, what am I to do with them?

I love riding my Kawasaki! On Oahu, you can pretty much head in any direction and you're going to arrive at a beach. As I cut through the wind, I think about what kind of scene I feel like today. Every beach has a different personality. Mostly, I want some sun. But am I in the mood for the people watching at Waikiki, the gay scene at Queen's Surf, the clear waters of Makaha? Or maybe I feel like the big waves of the North Shore?

I'm struck by the thought that this is not exactly the time to be aimlessly wandering around Oahu. Here I am with no sense of direction in my life and I'm wasting time meandering to the beach!

Then again, maybe some kind of magic will find me. I don't exactly have a lot of faith in my planning skills right now, since I was so off base with my ice cream company's business plan.

I guess I've never been one to research a path before taking it. Out of high school, I skipped college—against the advice of just about everyone—so that I might embark upon my own quest to be a rock video artist. I watched Prince in the film Purple Rain about six times and decided *that's* who *I* want to be.

I saw it again recently, and now I'd say it's one of the worst films ever made. But back then, to me, it was up there with Citizen Kane and The Wizard of Oz. I could have watched it forever.

I bought tens of thousands of dollars of electronic music equipment and basically built my own studio. I had no working knowledge of the music industry. No singing lessons. No lessons in song writing. Just a delusional dream.

Then I got married. *That* was a bright move—considering *I'm gay!* At the time, believe it or not, I just didn't realize it. My capacity to live in complete denial of practical reality is absolutely astounding to me. I just run as fast as I can with whatever strikes my fancy, and, usually, end up going straight off a cliff!

In an admonishing tone, the voice of Khaki man calls out to me in my mind. "Derek." I know. I'm not going to be mean to myself anymore.

In Kahala, I get off the H1 freeway and stop at a red light. Kilauea Avenue. This is my last opportunity to turn toward any of the town beaches. If I continue on straight ahead, I'll have to hit the beaches on the windward side.

Makapuu sounds nice. It'd be farther than I'd planned, but definitely quite beautiful. Or I could turn right now and go to Queen's Surf...Hmm...Makapuu? Or Queen's Surf? Why is every decision I have to make so damn *hard* for me lately?

Two Japanese girls pull up in a convertible in the lane to my right. The driver leans out the window and says, "Excuse me!" I turn to her, and she asks, "Do you know how to get to Makapuu?"

The traffic signal turns green. I have no time to explain. All I can say is, "Follow me! I'm going there!"

The view, as I round the bend, just after Hanauma Bay, is stunning. A deep blue waterscape dotted with sparkling whitecaps stretches out before me. For the last fifteen minutes, the girls have been following behind me. I enjoy feeling useful, helping them get where they want to go.

At the beach entrance, I hold up my right arm, and with my finger pointed out, wave them in. I park my motorcycle in a shady spot, not far from the entrance and wave to them as they drive on past, in search of a parking spot.

As I walk across the beach, a familiar voice calls out my name: "Derek!" It's my friend Richard! Richard is a very successful channel. He channels an entity called Ecton.

Richard has written several books and often travels to work in Japan. He was once featured on the Phil Donahue Show.

Many of my friends work for themselves, so they can (and do) make time for the beach during the middle of the day.

Hey, I wonder if the girls in the convertible led *me* here, as opposed to the other way around?

Richard and I frolic in the water for a while, stumble back onto the beach, then flop down on our towels. Lying belly side down, we draw in the sand with our fingers and talk. "Richard, I'm kinda freaking out."

"About what?"

"I've been having these coincidences. Like...I think things, and then they happen. It's a little creepy. Just this morning I asked what functions signs and coincidences serve, and I received an answer already on the way over here."

I tell Richard about the Japanese girls, the wall painting of stars, the ice-burning angel and the man in the khaki pants on Mars. "And I keep looking at the clock at 10:40, Richard. It doesn't seem to matter which clock it is—it could be any of mine or someone else's—but I will know when it's 10:40, because I'll look at the clock at exactly that time. Not 10:39. Not 10:41. But 10:40. I'm seeing it on bumper stickers, bar codes, telephone numbers, you name it. It's like I've got this 1040 connection inside me, or like the number is alive trying to say something to me."

"I have a friend who sees eleven eleven."

"A lot of people see numbers. I've been reading this book on signs but 1040 is not in it. Remember I told you about the session I had with that psychic?"

"Yeah."

"Well he said I was going to be getting these signs; that this council of guides was watching over me. I think it's happening."

"You're getting tuned in Derek. That's very cool."

"He said that if I ask them for help they'll send it. I'm pretty sure they're sending signs to me, Richard, but I want to know what they mean! I know that signs are supposed to point the way, so I tried playing this game. I asked The Council to specifically help explain what 1040 could mean by the way it next appeared to me. I thought I might glean something from the circumstances under which the number showed up."

"I gotcha. That's clever."

"So this week, my friend Sue picks me up for a day-hike into the mountains. We set off from my house and— you know how I am with directions—I let her do the driving. Well we got to talking, and I guess she got distracted or something. Suddenly she realizes she's taken the wrong route. 'You'll have to turn around,' I tell her. She says, 'Okay, I'll just turn around in one of these driveways.' She pulls into a driveway, and as we back out, I see the address on the mailbox is 1040! Then I realize—it means *Turn Around!* I'm somehow going in the wrong direction."

"Can I share something with you that just popped in for me, Derek?"

"Sure."

"You think this has something to do with your ice cream business?"

"Oh my God. That hits me like a laser beam. Yes. Probably. I have to turn my plan around. I'm going in the wrong direction."

"It certainly seems it."

"But, how can that be, Richard? I *created* that company. It's my baby. I loved that business."

"Do you love it now?"

"No. Not really."

"I mean, how many more signs do you want? Your freezer burnt down, Derek!"

"Yeah. I can't imagine getting clearer signs than what I've been getting. I'm in *way* over my head, Richard. I'm completely aware now—you need millions of dollars to run and grow this kind of operation. You can't do it small time."

"Maybe the Universe has better things in store for you."

"Failure is a doorway to success? I hate platitudes like that. I don't wanna fail!"

"Yeah but they're true. They say most millionaire entrepreneurs have declared bankruptcy."

I take a deep sigh, and gaze at sand falling through my fingers. "I'm thinking about doing psychic readings, professionally," I say.

"I think that's a great idea."

"You do?"

"Sure. I think you're perfect for it, Derek."

"You think I can do it?"

"Totally. Of course you can. I've got a question for you."

"Okay."

"Yesterday morning I saw, what appeared to be, a locust out on my lanai. It just sat there staring at me, which in itself is not that unusual, but I'd never seen a locust in Hawaii before. Here's the creepy part. I had forgotten about it and gone about my day. Later that night, in the *exact same spot*, I found a scorpion—also staring at me. It's just too coincidental. I think it's definitely a sign. I'm still freaked out by it. What do you think they want from me?"

"It *is* pretty coincidental, Richard. I agree—it must be a sign. I would see insects as a sign to take a look at what bugs you." God, *I* ought to know. "A scorpion's stinger is always ready to attack. Here's a question— Are you seeking revenge on anybody?"

"Little old me?"

"I know, you're too sweet for revenge, Richard. Let's think...Locusts may be harmless individually, but en masse, they will deplete a crop bare in no time. They are a symbol of massive destructive power. You may have only seen a harmless cricket, because I don't know if Hawaii has locusts. But you *interpreted* it as a locust, so therefore I'll interpret it as one.

The reason you see this incident as a sign is that the bugs appeared in the exact same spot. They must have a shared meaning. Or maybe they want us to fuse their meanings together. A Scorpion is the symbol of Scorpio...Do you know a Scorpio who is depleting your energy?"

"Oh My God! Bingo! Boy does that strike home. Yes! I don't want to go into it right now, but there's this guy I know, a Scorpio, and he's creating some drama that's starting to spread over into my world."

Proof

December 18, 2003

Late Afternoon

My journey in meditation to the planet Mars has stayed in my thoughts. I have yet to experience a waking dream as vivid and symbolically rich as that meditation, but each journey offers me something. I have been reading "Opening to Channel" by Sanaya Roman and Duane Packer for more insight on meeting spirit guides. It's been a big help.

Sometimes, when I'm conversing with my guide, I just feel like I'm talking to myself. How am I to know I'm really talking with my spirit guide? How would I recognize wisdom?

I've never felt that I ever truly silenced my mind. And I've let go of trying to do that. The reason most people have trouble achieving thoughtlessness in meditation is that deep within our unconscious we believe in Descartes' philosophical statement, "I think therefore I am." To have no thought is like death to the ego. The conscious mind is afraid of it.

Sitting in my meditation chair, I go through a ritual I've developed of relaxing one group of muscles at a time, from my feet to my head. I feel my body as both heavy like lead, and light like helium. It's strange, but I can feel both are true at the same time.

In my imagination, a white flower—this time with a red stamen—presents itself to me. I suspect it's a portal so I allow myself to become transfixed by it. I've learned that if I let a symbol mesmerize me, it will unlock the door to a place in a psychic reality.

I'll have to look up the significance of the colors red and white. I'm thinking of Alice in Wonderland, The Queen of Hearts. The stamen turns from a cranberry red to something darker, like blood. Blood cells are red and white. I am blood now. Yes, to be sure, I am my blood. I'm flowing through my veins. I am speeding through a tunnel of raspberry, purple, blue and black. It's a like being in a kaleidoscope.

"I have five principles I'd like share with you," I hear a deep voice say. I'm startled by this voice, which sounds familiar and reassuring. I'm trying to ascertain if he's Arnold's guide or the guy in khaki pants I met on Mars. "I think you will find them invaluable on your quest, Guiding One."

There is no face to go along with this voice. It's coming from the blood. "I don't know these five principles you're talking about," I telepathically reply.

"Then let me share them with you."

"Are you my Spirit Guide? Why don't you show yourself?"

"I will respond to the first question by asking who *you* are. Can you tell me?"

"I'm Derek."

"Really? Prove it."

"What do you mean, prove it?"

"Can you prove it?"

I am trying to figure out how I can prove I am who I am to him, but for the life of me I'm stumped. I can't exactly pull out my driver's license. It doesn't seem like it would serve as a valid ID here.

The voice says, "Can we move on to the five principles now?"

"Yes, sure. It's just nice to introduce yourself, don't you think?"

"I don't carry a specific name," he says.

"You don't?"

"People know me in different ways, I go by many names. You will come to name me by different names too."

"Really?"

"Haven't people called you by different names?"

"Yes, come to think of it. My brother calls me Bones, my friend Sue calls me Big D, there's my childhood name, Tim—"

"As to why I don't show myself, I can come to you in a specific form, as I did in our last session..." (He seems to be referring to Mars. So he *is* the khaki pants guy!) "But I feel that however I present myself to you today would distract from my purpose. It'll only cause you to ask more questions. Am I right?"

"I guess so, but as my spirit guide, don't you have a responsibility to—"

"So I prefer to remain invisible for now. Tell me, do you control how any of the people in your life present themselves to you? Do you have any say in that?"

"No, not really."

"Exactly. And does a father talk to his six year old child about his sex life?"

"Hey! This is Spirit Guide talk? No, of course he doesn't. Why are you asking me that?"

"Why doesn't a man talk to his six year old child about his sex life?"

"Because it's not appropriate for the kid's stage of development. And he has no context or ability to assimilate that information yet."

"That's the idea. Can we go on now?"

"Why are you so frustrated and impatient with me? Shouldn't a Spirit Guide be gentle and kind?"

"You expect gentleness and kindness, do you? What else do you expect about me? You want to see a halo over my head? You want me to have a long beard? How about a staff?"

"No, you can be whoever you want."

"Really? That's nice of you."

"I get all your points, okay? You don't have to beat me over the head with them."

"I don't? Ha! I'm going to remember that!"

We sit in silence for a moment as I process our exchange. This guy's a piece of work. I notice there is a metallic color swirling through the blood now. I'm not sure what to make of it. It might not have been metal, but it sure seemed it. Just as I'm about to ask him about it he says, "The five principles I offer for your consideration are: Patience, Dedication, Imagination, Humor and Strength."

A Necessary Procedure

December 27, 2003

Mid Morning

I am in the tackiest office I have ever seen, surrounded by faux wood paneling that should have been banned a long time ago. Three other people sit in a row alongside me. We look like errant students sitting outside the principal's office.

I don't want to admit that I have anything in common with these people, but I can't help noticing we all have greasy hair. Why didn't I shower this morning?

A picture of the Hawaii state governor hangs incongruously alongside an old Wyland poster on the wall opposite us. Four rows of cardboard filing boxes are stacked nearly to the ceiling. In the corner, a coffee maker warms half a tank of thick sludge on a small wooden table. A cracked Chinese teacup stuffed with sugar packets, creamery powder and red straws is wedged beside a vase of assorted plastic flowers. Only half the ceiling has tile.

A geeky man wearing square, black-framed glasses and a blue oxford shirt opens a door to my right and calls out, "Derek Calibre?"

"That's me." As I walk into his office, I have the thought that sometimes in life, we have to go through unpleasant yet necessary procedures. This must be similar to what it feels like for a woman to have an abortion; a strange combination of failure, shame and self-empowerment.

The man sits at his desk and asks, "How can I help you?"

"I need to declare bankruptcy."

Learning Trust

The Hunter

January 13, 2004

Late Morning

Will, my acupuncturist, has the sound of gently lapping ocean waves playing from speakers beneath the table. A kind of lemon balm—something like scented rose geranium—is wafting through the air. I am stuck all over with needles again.

Will says acupuncture isn't a one-time thing; that I need to come to consecutive weekly visits in order for me to see results from his work. I think he's right. I've only come sporadically over the last few months. This visit makes my forth in as many weeks and my strength is coming back. I'm becoming accustomed to our sessions.

I have no idea how long I've been laying here. I don't feel my body anymore. I can't sense the table either. Does everybody have this experience? Or just me? I actually look forward to the feeling, even though it scares me a little.

All is black in my imagination as if I'm floating in a void. Suddenly, a man's hairy face appears about four inches from my eyes. He has a huge nose and deeply set eyes. Though the face frightens me terribly, my body is paralyzed. I feel powerless. I can't run from it.

The face disappears momentarily; then appears again, like a reflection in nearly still water. It's so hairy it's practically like a dog. "A wolf, actually," the face says in reply. "I come from the family of wolves," he adds. "But I am also man." It's the voice of the man in khaki pants, but now he has a face. I feel like I'm being hypnotized. He says, "I am a Master of Wind."

I think of the wind chimes I have outside my front door. Telepathically, he confirms he'll send messages to me by blowing them at certain times. "I will present myself to you in many guises," he says.

I can't help questioning if this guy is my spirit guide. I know he's explained he is my guide, but he's a figment of my imagination! I want more definitive proof. I ask, "How do I know you're my spirit guide?"

He replies, "How do you know you're you?" Jesus, here we go again. I still don't know how to answer that question. After a moment he says, "I'll leave you my calling card."

Spirit guides have professions? "What do you do?" I ask.

"I'm a hunter," he replies.

I am taken aback by this. For a moment, we just float in space a few inches from one another. His eyes are warm. They look like a man's eyes. His nose is long, like a wolf's. I'm a little intimidated, but only because he's so different.

This doesn't make any sense. I'm against hunting. "But I'm against hunting," I say.

"Well, I don't know what to tell you," he responds, shrugging his shoulders unapologetically. "It's my work. It always has been."

Changing the subject, he says, "See this round, church window?" I begin to see it in my imagination. It's made of stained glass, with bright panes of orange, yellow, blue and green. In the center of it, I can see arrows pointing east and west. He says, "You built a nave at this spot a long time ago, Earth time."

Another voice abruptly calls out to me, "Derek? I'm ready to take the needles out now." It's Will. He's hovering right over me.

"I was dreaming, Will."

"It seems it. Where'd you go?"

"Uh...Outer space I guess. Or maybe inner space, I don't know."

"Uh huh." Will quickly moves around my body, taking out his needles.

"I met a wolf man."

"Really."

"Sounds a little crazy, doesn't it? But he said some things that... Well, they were mysterious but it felt like they might mean something. I don't know."

"Okay Kiddo," he says, ignoring me. Will hands me a bottle of Chinese herbs and adds, "Ten of these, mid-day and evening. We'll see how you are next week."

"Thanks Will." He throws back the curtain that encloses his acupuncture table and exits with a flourish as if he was Dracula. Will is getting more dramatic every day.

I get dressed, leave Will's office, and head over to my motorcycle. "You built a nave at this spot a long time ago," the wolf man said. What the hell is a nave? I should know that. Is it a stone room? A part of a church? I'll have to look it up when I get home.

As I head out onto the freeway I enjoy the feeling of the wind in my face. The wind is so strong that if I open my mouth it flaps my cheeks.

What if a bug flies into my mouth!? I continue on home with my lips together. "Master of Wind," he said. He'll send me messages from the wind? Maybe. But how the hell is he going to do that?

The oncoming head wind ripples my shirt, causing it to flap at my body. All of a sudden I notice I have an itch at the center of my chest, which becomes sharp and pronounced. Did a bee get caught in there and sting me?

I take my left hand off the handlebars and lightly scratch the area. The itchy feeling gets worse. Oh My God! Will left a needle in me! There's a needle in my chest!

After a few miles, when I am nearly home, I remember the voodoo doll I saw with my psychic eye in Uma's reading. Acupuncture. *I'm* the pin cushion! I remember thinking she'd get stuck with a pin. Now here it is, happening to me. In a weird way, I kind of feel like this is a validation of my psychic vision. Maybe some of the things I see for my clients are meant for me.

Once I'm in my driveway I get off my bike and gingerly take my shirt off. I can't believe I have to pull the needle out. Terrified, as quickly as I can, I do it.

Thank God. I got through *that* without dying. I'm such a wimp!

It was an honest mistake. I think Will is a brilliant acupuncturist. His treatments have definitely helped me. I'll keep going to him.

I never thought of *myself* having acupuncture treatment when I had the psychic vision of the human figure being stuck with pins. If I was psychically seeing my own acupuncture experience with Will, then I'm left to think there is some deeper message here for me. Otherwise why would my psychic mind have picked this particular incident to look at from all others? It must have done so for a reason. It didn't seem to mean anything to Uma, at least at the time.

Will forgot a needle in me. The meaning could be—keep your mind on what your hands are doing. Or it could be a sign to keep getting the acupuncture. I don't know.

For a couple of hours, I clean the house and repot some plants. My mind is mostly occupied with my bankruptcy filing, how it effectively ended my journey with my ice cream business. Suddenly, my chimes ring, and I remember the wolf-man. I never looked up the word nave! I grab the dictionary off my bookshelf, and start flipping through the pages.

For some reason I'm guessing a nave is a small prayer room. Maybe I'm wrong. I lick my middle finger and turn the pages. Naan...nagging...naughty...Here it is—nave. "The principle longitudinal area of a church, extending from the main entrance to the chancel, usually flanked by aisles of less height and breadth: generally used only by the congregation." Not a small room for prayer; a big one.

He said, "You built a nave at this spot a long time ago, Earth time." I built a church? Does he mean that literally? Or is he suggesting I built a following, like a congregation of people? I wonder.

Late Evening

Lying in bed, I can't help but think about the wolf-man. Why are spirit guides always wolves, or eagles, or bears? I expected someone different. I don't know who, but I didn't expect a wolf. Have I simply tapped into some typical representation of a spirit guide that I might have read about in a Native American book?

My nightstand holds an eclectic selection of reading material. Most of the books are non-fiction, the kind you don't have to read from front to back. I like to read from wherever I happen to open them. There's a book on tarot, another on dreams, some Jung. A book my father gave me called "Ariadne's Clue—A Guide to the Symbols of Humankind," by Anthony Stevens, catches my eye.

Without thinking, I open the book to a place somewhere in the middle. The chapter heading stuns me. It reads, "The Hunter."

Stevens describes The Hunter as "an archetypal symbol of great power and significance", and reminds the reader that hunting has been man's primary activity for most of our existence as a species. He suggests that civilization has been in a long evolutionary process of harnessing man's propensity to hunt for "the service of Church and State."

Wolf-man led me here, definitely. It's too coincidental! I flip through a few more pages, and my eyes stop on a page entitled, "The Mental Cathedral."

Here Stevens recounts the work of archeologist Steven Mithen, who describes four areas of intuitive knowledge that evolved from our ancestral hunter-gatherer existence; "'intuitive psychology', 'intuitive physics', 'intuitive biology', and 'intuitive language'."

Stevens writes that Mithen uses the symbolic image of a cathedral to illustrate his concept, whereby "the nave" represents general learning and intelligence, and the numerous side chapels stand for more specific intuitive domains.

I can't believe I've stumbled upon a reference to a nave, as associated with a reference to a hunter!

Symbolic Reality

January 22, 2004

Early Afternoon

Over the last few weeks my spirit guide and I have continued to meet in meditation. And I have continued to question him as to whether or not he really exists. His answers have been vague.

As I enter into a trance-like state of mind, I'm determined to settle this once and for all. In my meditation chair, I relax my body, and draw my attention to the center of my being. After some moments of silence, he says to me, "I am separate from you, and yet we are one, Guiding One." He keeps calling me Guiding One. I wish he would stop. It sounds a little ridiculous.

I sit with his statement about our being separate from one another, yet one, for a while. Sensing my confusion, he asks, "How do you understand something?"

"I don't know...experience?"

No reply. He seems to prefer asking questions over offering answers. I'm tired of it. "Why the hell do you ask me questions without providing the answers to them!? I just want to know you're not a figment of my imagination, that's all!"

"Dear Sir!" he replies in a flustered manner and with a British accent. "Might I be released from this constant inquiry into the truthfulness of my orations?"

Suddenly he's taken on a form of speech as if he were from the 18th century. He is clearly upset. He's never addressed me as "sir" before. And what's with "oration"? That's not a word I would ever consciously use. I'm not even sure I've ever even heard of it, though I think it must mean speech.

My awareness tells me that these last thoughts of mine are analytical in nature; they come from my conscious mind, and are not of an intuitive quality at all. I've left the meditation.

Where is that place that I meet my guide in meditation? What would I call it? "Symbolic Reality," a calmer voice in my mind says. Symbolic Reality. That sounds like it fits. I like it.

Getting up from the chair, I head to the dictionary for clarification on the word oration. I run my finger down the page. Here it is—"Oration; a formal speech, especially given on the occasion of an academic exercise." Hmm.

All afternoon, I mope around the house, feeling worthless. I have *no income!* There's no way I'm going to get a job. I've been working for myself for far too long to be working for somebody else. Being my own boss is all I know!

But I need money now!

What a screw up I am. I skip college, waste my twenties waiting tables, and then squander my thirties in some pie-in-the-sky *ala mode* business venture. Now here I am—nearly forty and I have NOTHING! No retirement savings. No house. No credit.

I'm DOOMED!

The phone rings. It's my friend, Matt. We talk for a while about old times working in the restaurant business. Before getting off the phone, he accepts my invitation to come up to the house for a beer after he gets off work.

Early Evening

My lanai is the perfect spot to watch the sun setting on the ocean. The horizon appears to be a perfectly straight line. I wonder how high up a person has to go in the sky before seeing the curvature of the earth. Matt and I watch commercial jetliners take off and land at Honolulu International. They look like flies from up here.

"My life is so surreal, Matt. I'm not entirely sure what's happening to me, but I've been having these psychic experiences. They're not meaningful visions or anything, but they're real to me."

As I say this, a voice in my head says, *what do you mean they're not meaningful?*

Matt sips his beer and lights a cigarette. He's a good listener. I trust him to support me in my psychic journey.

"I've been meeting this spirit guide in meditation and he's been having me look up words in the dictionary." I sound like I'm losing it. I look into Matt's eyes for signs he thinks I'm cracked, but he doesn't show any.

"I think I'm under this spirit guide's tutelage," I continue. "About a month ago, I woke up with the number twelve in my head. I don't know why. One of the psychic exercises I've been doing is to write down my first thoughts on waking, and then see if they correspond to my day in any way.

"All I had was this number, twelve. I didn't think anything would come of it.

"I went down stairs, made my morning coffee, and pulled my daily tarot card. The daily tarot card is another exercise I've been doing. Anyway, I get the Hanged Man, card number twelve. My tarot book says it's about being a victim, says I need to surrender and sacrifice. The way I see it, I've *already* surrendered, wouldn't you say?"

I'm fully aware I'm venting here. I don't think Matt is suffering by listening to me, but I feel like I'm whining. I just have to process this.

"Then," I continue, "I open my mailbox to find a twelve month calendar—a gift from my Australian friend, Karen. Along with it she includes a note written on a postcard. You're not going to believe this. The postcard is a Christmas advertising card from Gloria Jeans Coffee. It reads, 'Twelve Days of Coffee, Twelve Days of Tea.' I'm not kidding, Matt! I'll show it to you." I run in to the kitchen to get the postcard.

"D, I'll have another beer," he calls, as I head into the kitchen. I grab the postcard, and bring out two more beers from the fridge.

"Amazing," he says, taking the postcard from my hands.

"I'm not done. It gets better. The next night I was at Doris and Roy's for dinner. The topic somehow came to ancestors. Roy mentions ancestors.com, a web site where you can access historical information for a nominal subscription fee, 'like, twelve dollars,' he says. Then, Doris hands me a box of twelve note cards. She's always giving me stuff she acquires but can't throw away. When I get home, I have a voicemail message from this woman who wants me to work as a psychic at her New Year's Eve party. I'm terrified to do it, of course, but I called her back the next morning.

"Her secretary answered, saying she wasn't in. 'She doesn't usually get in to the office until around twelve,' she said. Then I think, New Year's Eve; the whole point of that holiday is to toast in the New Year—at twelve o'clock! Matt, am I making too much of nothing? Because if I am, then please tell me."

"It's pretty bizarre, D."

"Thank you! All this happened within two days! I couldn't stop seeing the number twelve.

"This kind of thing is happening to me all the time, Matt. And people don't understand. Some of my friends are listening to this thinking, 'Uh huh. You're nuts, Derek.' My friend Jackie dreamt I died the other day. Either I am going to die or I'm changing so much that the Derek she knew is, for all intents and purposes, dead. And that's how I feel; that life as I know it is dying."

"Everybody loves you, D. You don't gotta worry about that, man."

"Thanks Matt. I appreciate you saying that."

We gaze out at the ocean for a while. The sun is a bold orange, low down in the sky. I say, "People keep asking me if I can turn it off."

"Turn off what?"

"Being psychic. They assume I can see through everybody or something: that I can walk down the street seeing people's deepest darkest secrets, and I can't. I find it a bizarre question. And yet...I don't know...maybe I can't turn it off. I couldn't turn off twelve if I tried. We notice what we notice in life, right? It's like my antenna is being tuned to a different radio station or something. I don't want to turn it off, Matt."

"Why would you want to, D? You got something special. It's got to be leading somewhere. You've always been someone to listen to. I can't put it into words but plenty people would listen to what you have to say, man."

"You think?"

"Definitely."

Evening is rapidly descending upon us. "It's like being in a front row balcony seat up here on the mountain," Matt says.

"Yeah."

A peaceful breeze blows. My chimes let out two soft notes.

The Psychic Guy

February 18, 2004

Morning

The sky is a beautiful pale blue, the clouds, so well painted they look real. This scene serves its function well; it soothes me, even as Alan, my dentist, drills into my teeth. I'm going to suggest a ceiling like this to Will for his office.

So clouds represent peace. I must bear that in mind for my meditations and readings. Psychic messages seem to come in symbolic fashion. Since I've been studying them, everywhere I go, I notice the functionality of symbols. Exploring their meanings is like learning a new language.

I trust Alan implicitly. As a kid, I never liked our family's dentist. That guy had bad teeth, and always produced a fake, sinister-looking grin just before boring into my mouth. He seemed to enjoy inflicting pain on his patients.

Alan, by contrast, is gentle, his smile, white and reassuring. He employs excessive safety measures, which I find comforting. For example he makes you hold a child's beeper which you can sound off should you feel any pain. He's got Tweety Bird, Daffy Duck and a bunch of others. Today I have Road Runner. It's a psychological tactic, of course. But it works. It says, *See? Any kid can do this.*

I only hold the toy to placate Alan though. I know I won't feel any pain while I'm in his hands— even if I am undergoing a drastic procedure. I always leave Alan's office feeling uplifted.

"We all love your ice cream, Derek," he says through his mouth mask. I have a square piece of rubber in my mouth, that Alan calls a dam, so I can only respond by rolling my eyes. I use this code, which I'm hoping he'll figure out one day. A clockwise roll of my eyes means yes. Counter clockwise, no. It's a stupid game on my part. But hey, you've got to entertain yourself in the dentist's chair somehow.

99% of the population has never heard of my ice cream company. Many of the 1% who have heard of it know me as the founder. From the beginning, they've followed my story. They rooted for me like their favorite underdog, as I strived to make my dream of being an ice cream mogul a reality. For some of these people, that I've moved on is simply too tragic to bear. For them I've been a symbol that their entrepreneurial dreams could also come true.

Everywhere I go I have to break it to them; "NO, I don't own the business anymore. YES, I have moved on."

"But you are The Ice Cream Mogul!" they'll cry. Then, with a concerned face, they'll ask, "What *happened*?"

Often I've had to go into a detailed explanation of the situation to help them cope. "Oh, after a while, the business got so tedious. You know, health regulations, insurance premiums...*EMPLOYEES,*" I'll say, with added stress, widening my eyes. Even people who don't own a business know employees are a burden. "Plus all the TAXES," I'll sneer, wrinkling my nose. "It's Just Not Me."

"And what are you going to do *now*!?" they'll ask, as if they couldn't possibly imagine.

At first, I eagerly shared the exciting story of the new life I'm considering for myself. "I am going to work as a psychic!"

I said this on more than a few occasions, and quickly learned that 'Derek, The Psychic Guy' was not going to be as favorably received as 'Derek, The Ice Cream Guy.'

Everyone loved meeting 'The Ice Cream Guy'. "Wow, you make ICE CREAM!? That's SO COOL! Do you make Strawberry Banana? I LOVE Strawberry Banana!"

But it's been typical, I've noticed, over the last few months, for people, upon hearing I'm now 'The Psychic Guy', to react with a somewhat fearful, often skeptical stare. Imagine how someone would react if you had to tell them, say, the bubonic plague was back and your doctors thought you might be infected. That's the face I've been getting as I tell people that I'm thinking of working as a psychic.

"Inuuan!" I scream through the dam in my mouth, though I'm trying to say insurance.

"Oh, I know! *Tell* me about it," Alan says. "Insurance... don't get me going." Alan knows all about it. Alan's a *real* entrepreneur.

As he bores away at one of my lower left molars I consider setting him straight about my business status. If I don't tell him I'm going to work as a psychic now, he'll have me down as 'The Ice Cream Guy' for another six months!

He goes on about insurance for a while, but I can't say anything with the damn dam in my mouth. As he works, I squirm uncomfortably in the imitation rabbit-fur chair covering— another of his comfort measures. Maybe I won't tell him I'm going to work as a psychic. He'll give me that dreadful look. I can't bear that look right now.

"Derek's going to be mercury free now," Alan says to his assistant in training (and me) as if we were five years old. "These fillings you've had are old, Derek. I'm glad you decided to replace them with these new ones. They've found that the mercury in older metal fillings leeches into your blood over time, so it's good we're taking these out."

"Aungh," I say, looking up at Alan, as his assistant sucks up my saliva. Alan's wearing a white face mask of course, and strange microscope glasses. Looking into the left lens, I see a distorted reflection of my mouth—a small red glob swirled with metallic gray.

Hey! I remember this from my journey in meditation! I saw metal in my blood.

Karma Cat

February 28, 2004

Late Afternoon

The smell of dank, stale man-sweat overwhelms me as I enter the YMCA's locker room. I find the scent both disgusting and appealing at the same time. It always sends me into a slight state of confusion.

Turning the corner, I run into Jerry, my friend Steven's old roommate. He doesn't look too good. I haven't seen Jerry in years. We only knew each other casually. He never disclosed to me he had HIV. But it's pretty obvious now that he has AIDS. Poor Jerry!

"Derek!"

"Hi Jerry! Wow, I didn't expect to see you here."

"I'm staying here. I just got out of the hospital."

"Oh, Jerry..."

"It's not that bad. I just wish I could eat! I would love a burger, but it just can't happen."

We change our clothes and talk. He tells me of his recent visit to see his family in Philadelphia. How he had to say goodbye to his mother, each of them knowing they would never see one another again. His sister disowned him a long time ago. She could never accept that he was gay, and never bothered to stop by the house while he was there.

Hearing Jerry tell me all this brings me to tears. Standing in my underwear, I start to cry.

"I've lost eyesight in one of my eyes," Jerry says with a smile. "If you see me bumping into things, it's cause I lost all my depth perception!"

My God, his spirit is still so bright! "Are you up for a walk with me," I ask?

"Sure, I can. Actually, I'll take advantage of you. You can help me with something in my car. It's parked along the Ala Wai Canal."

We finish getting dressed, and head out to Ala Wai Boulevard where Jerry leads me to an old beat up Chevy. "This is everything I own," he says, opening his hands out to the car. "I've been slowly divesting myself of all my stuff!" He opens the trunk and amidst snorkel fins, coffee cups, a pair of military camouflage pants and a small TV, he finds a quartz crystal about the size of my palm. "Here," he says, "I want you to have it."

"For me?"

"That's Froggy," he says. "Doesn't he look like a frog?" Turning it in my palm, he adds, "See the head and the two legs?"

"I do! It does look like a frog! Wow, thanks Jerry! What a surprise."

"I told you. I'm getting rid of all my stuff. I can't be hauling this shit around anymore. I don't have the energy. Hey, if you want something to eat, I'd join you."

"Sure, I'd eat, Jerry. I have time. I have all the time in the world these days."

"I know a place near here. And there's a cute shop around the corner from it I want to show you. Maybe I'll be able to stomach that burger."

We make our way up to a diner on King Street. The walk stretches Jerry to his limits. Once we're at the restaurant, he slumps into one of the plastic orange booths and collects himself for a few moments.

"Are you okay? We can take a taxi back."

"I'm fine. Just give me a minute." He stares at the table for a moment, breathing heavily. "I don't think I can handle the burger after all. You go ahead though. I'll just have tea."

My heart sinks. "Jerry, I couldn't possibly have a burger right now."

"Well, you gotta eat. You gonna not eat on my account? Don't be stupid."

I order Chicken Katsu. Every time Jerry takes a sip of his tea, he winces. We fall into silence. This wasn't the plan I had for tonight. I had no plans, but the way it's turned out gives me the feeling this whole evening's been specially orchestrated somehow— that Jerry's an angel playing tour guide.

He doesn't have much time left. Anyone can see that. God, he's living his last days out of the YMCA, and his car. I don't know what to talk about with him. I didn't realize it until now, but for those of us who aren't in the later stages of a terminal illness, every conversation we have is held under the premise that life is continuing on. I want to talk about the latest artist coming to town, emerging technologies, politics, a friend's graduation. But I can't get myself to talk about any of them—they all relate to the future in some way.

In this short time with Jerry, my empathy for his situation has shifted my view of the world. The salt-and-pepper shakers, the gravy stained waitress, the Formica counter—all these things are somehow more alive. I can't explain it.

"I'm getting kind of tired," Jerry tells me. "But I wanted to take you by this mystical shop before heading back. The guy who owns it is really cool. His name is Alec."

A block and a half down the street, Jerry stops in front of a beautifully lit little art gallery called Karma Cat. "Here it is," he says. Then he ducks his head and passes through a Japanese style curtain hanging in the doorway. I follow him inside and all my senses are instantly stimulated. *What a magical place!* The walls are painted a bold Chinese red. Candles and stained glass lanterns sparkle galore. The air is sweetened with a musky incense. We hear an Indian guitar, and occasionally, the pleasant chirping of two finches flitting about in a bird cage hanging above a cash register. The place is filled with an eclectic assortment of curios, all tastefully arranged. There are cards, necklaces, paintings, dolls, lamps and masks.

Behind the counter, a local guy fits a yarn wig onto a paper mache head. He's youthful, thirty-something, with shoulder length hair and a soft, sweet disposition. He's wearing a red-and-black-checkered flannel shirt and women's chinos. Gotta love artists! "Alec, this is Derek," Jerry says.

Alec and I say, "Hi," in unison, to each other, our eyes smiling.

Jerry and I tool around Alec's shop for a few minutes. After making a complete circle of the place I tell Alec, "I could spend hours in here."

"Please do!"

I tell him, "You know what I could see in here? A Tarot reader."

Alec's face brightens. "I love it."

"You do?" Derek, why did you say that? Now he's going to ask you if you read Tarot cards. And you *don't* read Tarot cards! Not yet. Not professionally!

"Do you read the Tarot?" Damn, I knew it! You opened the door, Bonehead.

"Uh...yeah. Kinda. I've been learning."

"You want to do a reading on me and we'll see how it goes?"

"Now?"

"Sure, why not?" I turn to Jerry to check how he's doing but he's engrossed with a small water fountain.

"Oh, well, I don't have my tarot cards." I tell him.

"I have some."

"You do?" Jesus, I don't believe this.

"I'll show them to you."

Alec turns around and fishes through a drawer behind the counter. I make my way over to Jerry. "Hey Jerry, you think you can hold up for ten minutes while I give Alec a tarot reading?"

"Sure, I'm cool."

"Okay."

Gosh, this place could be perfect. Alec gets customers here. I could set up a table in the corner and work a couple of night shifts a few hours a week.

Moving back to the cash register, I discover that Alec has already set up a little table and two chairs behind the counter. He's laying down a sheer fabric on the table. It's printed with shooting stars and a moon.

Where did he get all this stuff? Within a minute he lights a candle, lays out a Ryder Waite Tarot deck and seats himself in one of the chairs.

How did this happen? I feel like I'm on a moving train I can't stop.

Here goes...I flip two cards; The Hermit and Temperance. For the life of me I can't think what they could possibly mean right now.

Oh! Temperance is that Art card, the one with fire and ice! "Alec, all these candles...You have to be careful not to start a fire."

"You see a fire?"

"No! No. Just be careful, that's all." Shit. This is already going badly. Help! These cards to mean nothing to me. I stare at them blankly. Nothing seems to resonate. Except, in my peripheral vision, a large star printed on the table cloth seems to shine quite brightly. A smaller star nearby twinkles more meekly. "I see a bright star..." Very good, Derek. Keep going. "And a smaller star that's not so bright." Yeah, that's what you are right now Derek—'not so bright.' What the hell are two stars supposed to mean? "The bigger star is shining ever more brightly. It's glaring, like the sun. It's overpowering the smaller star. It's blinding me. I can't look at it. I see you as the smaller star. It's trying to get noticed, but it can't compete." I look up at Alec and he has tears in his eyes. "What did I say Alec?"

"My father is the bigger star. I will never measure up in his eyes."

"Oh...I'm sorry." My God. That star business actually meant something to him. But of course! Sun and star. I read in my tarot book the symbolism of the sun is the father. A star is a small sun.

I think I'm supposed to leave him some wisdom on this subject at this point. But I don't know what to say! I give it my best shot. "Alec, the smaller star only seems small to us because we're so far away from it. The sun and the star are actually about the same size. But we have to move far away from the sun to see that. This huge sun that once seemed so powerful is really just a little star. Distance yourself and you can shine in your own right." Alec nods.

Hey, Derek, that actually sounded pretty good!

"Derek," Jerry calls from the customer side of the counter. "I'm getting kinda tired."

"Okay Jerry."

"You can do readings here, Derek. I mean, we'd have to work out terms or whatever, but I'm sure that won't be a problem. I like your energy."

God, it's like he can read my mind! "Really?"

"Yeah, I think you're really good."

"Thanks! Okay. Uh...I'll be in touch then!"

Jerry insists on walking back to the Y, where we stand for about a minute in a nice warm hug. The whole ride home, I'm on cloud nine.

I pull up to my house, turn off my motorcycle's engine and get off the bike.

From where I stand, on the top of Alewa Drive, I can see the lights of the airport, Aloha Tower and Honolulu's shipping piers. Everything is quiet. A light breeze blows. Looking up through the telephone wires, I see a dark blue sky sprinkled with a few faint stars. I know there are more stars up there, but the street lamp in front of my house glares so brightly it ruins the view. Why can't the state use something dimmer?

It is not lost on me that this is the basic shape of the image I was seeing in Alec's reading. I'm getting accustomed to seeing patterns like this. It's becoming almost like a game, where I try to match what I see in my imagination with a scene from reality.

As I ascend the steps to my front door I'm startled to see a huge frog sitting directly outside my front door. I've never seen a frog here. It's as if Jerry's crystal called it. Frog! You came to me!

Maybe, Maybe Not

March 3, 2004

Evening

"I've decided to call you Teacher," I say to my spirit guide.

"As you wish, Guiding One."

"Why do you call me Guiding One?"

No answer. I guess I know the answer to that already. He won't answer questions for which I already have answers. Nor will he respond to questions I ask twice. "Am I talking to myself?"

"Maybe. Maybe not."

"That's not a very straightforward answer."

"Your question isn't answerable as yes or no."

"How can I know for sure you're my spirit guide?"

"You will know when you stop asking that question."

"So I just have to assume?"

No answer.

"Can I ask you about my boyfriend, Ken?"

"What about him?"

"I've been wrestling with whether or not to proceed with the relationship, or break it off."

"What are the pros and cons?"

"Well, I know this sounds silly, but the first thing that comes to mind when I think about what I love about him is that he likes to cook."

"A person who likes to cook shows great qualities—discipline, patience, sensuality, creativity... To like that he cooks does not seem so silly to me."

"He's also Chinese, which presents a whole set of problems in itself. We're not even from the same culture! And he's twelve years younger than me. His English isn't proficient. We're on different planes. Frankly, it's hard to communicate. Should I be in a relationship with him? Or not? Because I'm really wrestling with it."

"You have a lot to work out as far as staying in a relationship goes. I think you know that. For now, it might be helpful to simply ask yourself if you enjoy him when you're in his company. If you don't, leave."

"I do enjoy myself when I'm with him."

"Well, to enjoy someone means to be IN YOUR JOY with them. Did you know that? IN JOY is what enjoy means."

The way he says this makes me think he's quoting from the dictionary. I suppose it makes sense that enjoy means to be "in joy," but I wonder how he knows it to be specifically defined that way.

"Go look it up if you don't believe me."

As soon as I get out of the meditation, I run to my den, and pull my dictionary off the shelf. Flipping through the pages, I scan through the e words.

Here it is—enjoy. Holding my finger under it, I read the definition, "enjoy—In joy." Below the definition is a sample sentence. It reads, "He enjoys Chinese food."

Plastic Clips

March 15, 2004

Early Evening

Alec's finches are sweetly chirping over by the register. He's set me up at a table by the window so passersby can see me. He's put up a curtain for privacy, and decorated the area with a crystal ball and candles. It's a bit fortune-teller-like for me, but it's his store to decorate as he wishes.

The client across from me is in a wheel chair. I try not to let this influence me in any way, but it's hard. I wonder if this guy works? Would he be on some sort of disability? I probably think that because he's in a wheelchair.

I sit in silence and glance down at the floor. Alec has some miscellaneous packaging supplies stored discreetly under a counter. My eyes move over them. One box reads *Plastic Clips*.

I'll just ask him. I can't see everything for crying out loud. "What do you do for work?"

"I work at a plastics company," he replies.

Plastics. Damn, it was right in front of me.

Wolf Man Returns

March 21, 2004

Afternoon

My problem is, I want to please everybody. But only some people will be receptive to my psychic work. Others won't. That's just all there is too it. I'll have to accept it.

Last night, I was at a party. I met an acquaintance, a lawyer, who, upon hearing I'd started a business as a psychic, immediately said, "Oh, I don't believe in all that crap."

The conversation was closed. That really hurt.

I didn't know what to say. I certainly wasn't about to get into it with a lawyer. I would've lost the argument. But who's the presiding judge, anyway?

Me, I guess.

I'm *observing* something in all this psychic phenomena, and it's *real* to me! I enjoy Ken's Chinese cooking, someone in my head says to "go look up the word 'enjoy' in the dictionary", and the dictionary says, "He enjoys Chinese food". There *has* to be something that's connecting...But there's no evidence. All there is, is a mystery.

Derek, you are out of the mainstream now. You're off the grid.

Recently, I handed out my first psychic business card. I ran into a woman named Denise whom I met at a food show last year. She asked me how things were going at my ice cream company. Reluctantly, I told her about my new psychic work.

I was so pleased when she didn't give me that 'you have the bubonic plague' look.

Alec recommended a byline for my card: *Career, Relationships, and Decisions*. "That's what everyone is going to want to ask about," he said. I never thought about the kind of questions people would ask, but these topics sounded right to me, so I used them.

Sure enough, Denise looked at the byline and said, "I have a relationship decision to make. I have to come see you." I'm quite happy with my business cards!

I am currently perusing through the Self Help/ Spirituality section at Barnes and Noble. I've seen most of the tarot decks and angel cards they're selling. A new one, with a lion on it, titled, "Native American Animal Cards" calls my attention. Suddenly I remember a reading I did the other day in which I told a woman, "There are animal spirits all around you. They are old friends, and will offer help when you call them and acknowledge your connection with them." I felt like an idiot saying this. But as it turned out, my comment made complete sense to her. She proceeded to tell me about how much she loved animals—she had several rabbits, a few chickens, a horse, a cat, and two dogs.

I buy the deck and head over to the cafe for a cup of coffee. Opening the box, I contemplate the symbolism of the lion pictured on it. Stealth. Instinct. Courage. Pride.

The deck itself is inside the box; tightly wrapped in shiny cellophane. Upon pulling it out I'm startled to see a wolf pictured on the top card!

Excited, I attempt to examine him, but the florescent white ceiling lights shine so brightly, that it's hard to see his image clearly through the reflective cellophane. All I see is my own reflection in the plastic.

The image of my own face overlaid on the wolf's creeps me out a bit—Oh my God! The Wolf-Man. *His "calling card!"*

"I told you I would send my calling card." The words are telepathic, but clear in my mind. "Do you see yourself in me? Haven't you ever seen your father in yourself? Or yourself in your friends? I could not be me without you."

Suddenly I feel like I might be standing out in the crowd of cafe patrons around me. I look around the place to make sure no one is noticing me. That's what a wolf would do—crouch down into the thicket!

I cannot deny that this guide has come to me now. Why should I not acknowledge him as an Intelligent Being, separate from me? And yet why should I not see that I am also a part of that Intelligent Being?

Rolling Tortillas

March 24, 2004

Late Morning

I still don't get these psychic readings. Am I really supposed to make a living at this? It's so strange, people paying me to listen to what I hold in my imagination for them.

Enough clients have come to keep me doing it. But I am barely paying my rent on time. And I don't even have a sense I'm really helping anyone. *God, please let me know I'm on the right track.*

The woman in front of me looks at me expectantly. I feel her hanging on my every word. Recently, I've been letting myself think in a more dream-like fashion, especially in readings. Perhaps the surreal occurrences of late have had an effect on me.

My eye falls on a suitcase pictured on a postcard I have laid on the table. I've been collecting postcards and using them like tarot cards. The pictures are more relevant to our times than those on the regular tarot. And my clients identify with them better. There's no rulebook that says the tarot is the only authoritative oracle around. Why shouldn't a deck of postcards offer a telling glimpse into life?

"Are you going on a trip soon?"

"Yes," she replies.

Thank you, suitcase! Where are you going?

I close my eyes, and gaze into the gray and black shapes swirling behind my eyelids. The shapes settle into an outline of hands rolling something on a table, like a scroll...No, not a scroll, but like...Well, I can't tell what it is.

With my mind's hands, I reach out to feel it. The hands that roll the scroll are my own hands now. I'm a woman.

The item isn't paper at all. It's soft to me, with bumps and dimples in it. A ribbed condom?

Derek! You can't tell her you see that!

A puff of powder makes a small cloud around my hands. Oh! It's *dough*. Women in colorful skirts stand around watching me. The air is dry.

"I see you in a cooking class, learning to roll tortillas or something." The tortilla in my imagination turns into fabric. As the woman, I hold it up to my body. "You're going to buy some fabric to make an outfit or maybe hang as a tapestry."

"You're giving me chicken skin!" My client's exclamation pulls me back to reality. "I'm going to Mexico on a women's retreat..."

Uma's Confirmation

March 29, 2004

Late Evening

Before turning into bed I decide to meet Wolf-Man in meditation. "There are many shades of gray between black and white, Guiding One," he says to me. "You sometimes leave yourself little room for compromise. We think you might benefit by tempering your appointments with yourself."

Tempering my appointments? What the hell does that mean? I know tempering means to balance or modify, maybe accommodate. But appointments? Appointments are things you make with the dentist. And I don't have any! What an odd choice of words.

My cell phone rings from the upstairs bedroom, popping my meditative bubble. I am out of "the zone." I can't believe I forgot to shut off that phone!

I bolt out of my meditation chair, rush upstairs, and answer it. "Hello?"

"Derek, it's Uma. Do you remember doing a reading for me?"

"Yes! Uma. Hi."

"Derek, you're not going to believe this. Do you remember you told me I would go visit Portland? Well, my boyfriend just called to tell me he got accepted by this school in Portland. Originally it was his second choice, but now he's decided to *move* there. This was totally out of the blue for me.

I'm going on a scouting trip to help him look for an apartment. You were right!"

"Wow, that's great Uma!"

"I just wanted to give you the confirmation. You're good!"

"Thanks!"

I say goodbye, hang up, and practically bounce down the stairs. I'm so happy to hear I wasn't totally off base or crazy with Uma's reading. What a great feeling!

I guess sometimes the information coming through for the client will be unfamiliar to them. I'll have to learn to leave them the information that comes to me, and not be affected by their reaction to it.

In mentioning the possibility of Portland to Uma long before she would decide to go there, it seems I introduced an idea that she might not otherwise have considered. Was she *meant* to go to Portland in some grander design or destiny? I wonder.

Upon seeing the meditation chair I am reminded of Wolfman's words: "We think you might benefit by tempering your appointments with yourself."

What does he mean, "We"? Is this the council Arnold talked about? Everything is a mystery with my guide. I guess I like that. And maybe he knows this. What am I saying? Of *course* he knows this! He knows *exactly* how to arouse my curiosity.

His use of the word appointments definitely intrigues me. I race to the dictionary in search of the meaning. *God, it's like a game!*

Appalachian Trail...Appetency...Wait, what does appetency mean? "Appetency; *archaic* a longing or desire. • a natural tendency or affinity." Hmm, so many words, so little time. I guess you can't retire archaic words. We need them for when we read Shakespeare.

Appointments. I place my finger under it. There are eight definitions. Who would've guessed?

None of the first seven fit Wolf-Man's usage, but the eighth does. The meaning is archaic. This seems appropriate, now that I think about it, given the old style of speech he was using.

The eighth definition reads, "decree, or ordinance."

Hmm. A decree is like an edict or command. "We think you might benefit by tempering your appointments with yourself." It makes sense. He's suggesting that I be easier on myself. That's a familiar message. What a funny way to put it!

Lessons In Perception

Golden City

April 4, 2004

Late Morning

I intend to travel back in time today, to a past life. I don't know if we live successive lives, in time as we see it, but I like that idea. I believe our minds can transcend time and space as we perceive it. If I can experience what my calling was in a past life, then perhaps it will point the way to what I'm suited for in this life. The key stories of those times must be filed in my mind somewhere.

I've been working with a system, which I've assembled from a few books, to help me completely still my body. Instead of trying to silence my mind, I engage it. I give it the task of taking a toe-to-head tour of my body, consciously instructing each muscle group to surrender all effort. My feet and calves become heavy, like lead, as do my knees and thighs, and so on, right to the crown of my head.

I visualize myself transformed into, perhaps, a lake, or a tree – something from nature.

Having just now gone through my mental tutorial, I feel myself to be a giant, craggy rock. I take a moment to allow myself to *be* this rock, to get past the strangeness of it and settle into really feeling it. Parts of me are covered with a mottled black and green fungus. Oak leaves, woolly bear caterpillars, and soft fragrant mushrooms surround me.

I wonder if I will find myself in another country? Which year it will be? I've always had the impression I lived somewhere like the Irish countryside.

A voice asks, "Will you accept what is shown to you?"

"Yes," I reply, with a little apprehension, for the very question suggests that I may not want to believe the vision that is coming.

In my vision, I am presented a round stained glass window. The same one my guide once mentioned. Its panes are luminous, various shades of yellow, green, and blue. There's a spiral pattern to it, like a galaxy. It has become quite bright. I am descending into it, traveling at high speed through a bright yellow tunnel.

I am high up in a cloudless sky now, looking down upon an ancient city, a shining metropolis in the middle of the desert. Immediately, the place gives me a sense of wealth.

I feel like I'm in a movie. Many of the buildings have rounded rooftops. It's about four o'clock in the afternoon. Golden sunlight reflects beautifully off a huge, domed mosque. It looks like I'm in Arabia.

"It's a City," I comment.

"It's a *Golden* City," my guide replies.

"Yes, I see that."

"Are you surprised?"

"I thought I always lived in the country."

"No. This was your home." Again I notice the mosques are drenched in gold light. The streets, sidewalks and buildings are all sand toned. I don't see any other colors. "Let's find you," he says.

We float through the street at ground level, past a long line of people who are waiting to get into a temple. They are all troubled over one thing or another. They need a sense of hope, some healing, or understanding.

"Which one of them am I?" I ask.

Without answering, he takes me into the mosque, which is dark and refreshingly cool inside. A gray shaft of incense smoke is highlighted blue by a platinum beam of light pouring down from the ceiling. Tall candles flicker in the corners.

A robed healer sits atop a raised marble slab in the center of the room. One by one, people approach him from the long line outside. He seems to be dispensing some kind of spiritual guidance.

There's a blood-stained turban wrapped around his head as if he recently sustained a head injury. He sits in a semi-lotus position on a square pillow with his left hand held out, palm side up. I'm not certain if this hand is open in order to receive money or wisdom from the heavens.

"That's you, on the pillow."

"The *Turban Guy? That's me?*"

"Yes, that's you."

Everything is black. The vision is over.

After coming out of trance, and giving my journey some thought, I become somewhat suspect, and also afraid, of my past life vision. I can understand how I would be a healer or spiritual counselor of some kind, but not such a prominent one! And I don't like the part about the bloody turban on my head. *At all.* Does this mean I am to be wounded in some way? I'm wounded enough already! I hope I'm not in for more.

I like the idea of being busy, however. Turban Guy certainly had a long line of people waiting for him. I would hope for that. Something feels canned about the whole thing though. Am I really supposed to believe I was some guru, revered by thousands? Come on, give me a break.

"Tens of thousands, actually," Teacher comments in my head.

"Oh, come on! Why is everyone in past life visions some iconic figure, like Cleopatra or Alexander the Great? Didn't anyone wash dishes? Or run say, a watch repair shop? Or—"

"Why exactly did you ask to see a past life, Guiding One? I asked if you would accept the vision given to you. And you said yes, you would. Now it seems you are not so satisfied with it. Of course you washed dishes. But that is not the activity I chose to represent the essential work of this particular past life."

"It just seems implausible is all. I feel a little arrogant looking at it."

No comment. The conversation is over I guess. I should have known that delving into a past life would not be something to do lightly.

The whole point of this exercise was to reference a vision of my past life to serve as a guide for my future in this life. But I don't want to play the role I was shown! Especially if it means I have to have a bloody head injury!

I clean up around the house for a while, and do some dishes I'd left in the sink. Then I call my father, thinking he might have something to say about some of the symbolism in my journey.

"Jung spoke of the archetype of the Wounded Healer," he says. My father is always referring to Carl Jung, the Swiss psychiatrist. "The healer is aware of his own wounds as he meets with his patient. There is a conscious and unconscious transference of experience between therapist and patient that helps facilitate the healing process."

When you ask my dad for advice, you're going to get food for thought you can chew on for a week. Which reminds me, I'm hungry.

There's not much in my fridge; a door full of condiments and a few wrinkling vegetables. I hop on my motorcycle, and head down the mountain to do some grocery shopping, considering what options I have for eating out along the way.

I want something healthy, but I can't recall any place that serves a good portion of vegetables near my supermarket. There's that Thai place on Nuuanu, but I've eaten there a lot lately. There's Subway. No, I don't feel like a sandwich.

I wonder if I was a hunter in a past life? Did I forage for food, or grow it? I grew it, more likely. I can't imagine myself tip toeing through the woods with a bow and arrow.

A cat, running across the street, jars me from my daydream. As I catch my bearings I realize I've unconsciously driven the road I used to take to get to my ice cream plant. It's a route that snakes its way down the backside of the mountain, towards the airport. Now I'll have to take School Street to get downtown. *Derek, you can be so absentminded!*

Why do I always take the long way to get where I want to go?

As I wait at a traffic light at the bottom of the hill, I suddenly remember that there's a Chinese place just up the street. Chinese! *That's* what I feel like. *I knew there was a reason I came this way!*

Sometimes, following the unconscious mind can beat planning. I make a right, pull into the parking lot, get off my motorcycle and take off my helmet. The restaurant is called *Golden City.* A creepy, yet wonderful eeriness overcomes me. For about a minute, I just stand in my parking spot, staring at the sign.

A Chinese restaurant is a Chinese restaurant. Who remembers the names of them? I don't. I never consciously remembered the name of this place. I will *now*, though, that's for sure.

I enter the restaurant, somewhat zombie-like, and sit at a small table facing the lobby. The walls are painted a hue of lavender that belongs on a crayon. Two sorry carp with no place to swim watch me from their filthy fish tank.

A woman behind the counter presses ground pork and green onions into squares of dough with factory like efficiency. Behind her, cardboard trays from cases of soda are stacked to the ceiling. The owners recycle them as carry-out packages for family take out orders. What the Chinese lack in aesthetic values, they make up for in frugality.

To the right of the trays, hangs a poster of Buddha. He's seated on a square pillow in a lotus position with his left hand held out, palm side up.

Oh my God! What a fool I am. Here I ask for information about my past life and I get a psychic vision of *Buddha*? In a *Golden City,* no less. What kind of trick is this? Was I somehow duped by a mischievous sprite? It certainly feels like it.

I pull out my cell phone and dial Richard.

He answers in Japanese. "Moshi Moshi!"

"Richard, It's me. You're not gonna believe this..."

Early Afternoon

"I was trying to go to my past, but ended up going to my future somehow, Richard. I feel like Samantha's aunt on that old TV show, Bewitched."

"Which one was that?"

"The old aunt, who's magic always went haywire. She'd try to make a graceful entrance into the house, and would end up coming down the chimney."

"Aunt Hagatha?"

"Was that her name?"

"I think so. At least you're prettier!"

"Thanks."

"Derek, our guides have wonderful, ironic senses of humor. To me, the fact that he tied your spiritual path to our world in such a clever way says that you're clued in. He's given you confirmation of your talent in a sensitive and intelligent way. And maybe you had a past life working in a Chinese restaurant!"

"Well, I have actually, in this life. My first job was as a dishwasher in a Chinese restaurant in Rhode Island. And that's another thing. Why is everyone Cleopatra or Napoleon in past life regressions? No one's ever a dishwasher or a garbage collector."

"Aren't you going into the past to learn about the future? Why would you want to see something so mundane?"
"That's what my guide said."

"I would think a spirit guide would want to inspire you, Derek. These sessions are meant to influence us as to core talent. They reveal experience we can draw on. Look at it as finding out what's on your resume. In this type of vision, the messages coming through are going to be bold and symbolic. Don't take it so literally. In the meditation, you were essentially performing, which is something you've always wanted to do as an actor. The audience was the line out the door, waiting to see you. It conveys so much; reaching a lot of people, being respected..."

"What about the bloody turban, Richard?"

"Maybe you were dropped on your head as a kid!"

Big Island Girl

May 18, 2004

Morning

Hawaii's Big Island lies invitingly beneath me. My God, these islands are so beautiful!

Flights to the outer islands are often choppy. For the last few minutes, the plane has been bouncing fairly heavily. We hit an air pocket and everyone gasps. I can feel the other passengers praying for a safe landing. The flight attendants, thankfully, seem unfazed.

We land safely, and as our plane taxis off the runway I review how this trip became possible. Here I am, poor as dirt, flying to the Big Island. How? One of my clients is paying for it. Amazing. She wanted to buy a birthday present for her friend, and decided to give a psychic reading from me as the gift! I hope I'm worth it.

I asked God for a sign that I was on the right track with my work. I'm thinking this has to be it. How much more of a sign do I need?

Late Morning

The birthday girl is twenty-four, with long blond hair. She has a sultry air about her. She looks like she's been brooding over a problem. Her name is Karla, and she is, naturally, taken aback by my visit. Of her surprise gift, her friend only told her to be home, and ready for a mystery. I wonder if it was such a good idea to spring me on her like this.

Karla has the air of a queen about her. She greets me warily. I imagine her thinking, "*Who*, exactly, are *you*?"

A warm breeze moves through her house, which is small and casually furnished. Photographs, newspaper clippings and Hawaiian trinkets adorn the walls. Through the window I see a palm tree shake off some birds. A horse grazes in the yard next door. Resplendent mountains watch over everything.

Karla offers me a seat on a blue futon sofa. She then sits about five feet across from me, much higher up on a bar stool. We're not at all on the same level. She looks at me warily, as if I were an unfamiliar dog she'd just taken in.

"Come sit by my side," I suggest, patting the cushion next to me. She moves over and we each make ourselves comfortable.

From the short time I've been doing psychic readings, I've learned that, when I don't know what to say, something meaningful can be said by simply speaking. Whatever comes out of my mouth will very likely hit the mark.

From what I've observed, accurate psychic insights do not have to be said with any justification. They're not reasoned thoughts. In fact, they seem to come from an unreasoning mind.

Recently, I was reading for a woman who wanted some insight into this guy she was seeing. She didn't say much about him. Just, "I'm seeing this guy. We've been going together a few months. I like him a lot. I wonder what you see about it."

In preparing to answer her, I glanced off to the side, in a stance of reflection. My eye fell on a pair of window curtains, which happened to be printed with a maple leaf motif. Maple leaves remind me of Canada. It's completely irrational to think this curtain has anything to do with her boyfriend, but I had nothing else to go on, so I said, "The guy's Canadian?" And she said, "Oh my God. How did you *know* that?"

There is no rationale to this psychic business that I can see. It's a free-for-all.

I open Karla's reading by saying, "I see your mother as an angel." I say this for no logical reason. I say it because I feel that an angel helped coordinate my being here with Karla.

With shock and hostility, she rebuts, "*My mother!*? I HATE my mother."

Oh, God. *Please may this go well.* We have gotten off on the wrong foot. She's denied my statement about her mother a little too vehemently though. Maybe I am on to something.

She asks, "Can you tell me about my father?"

She is testing you, Derek. But I bet she's in the dark herself. I inquire within myself and, in my mind's eye, I see the Cheshire Cat from Alice in Wonderland. It appears, then, disappears. Appears, then, disappears again.

How weird. *That's* a representation of her father? And what of her mother?

This question about her mother is answered with an image of Snagglepuss, a Hanna-Barbera cartoon character from my childhood. Snagglepuss was a cat who was always hightailing it out of trouble. As soon as circumstances deteriorated around him, he'd say, "Exit, stage left!"

I open my eyes and gaze out the window at the horse in the neighbor's pasture. What a dumb, blank expression I must have on my face. What the hell am I supposed to do with *this?* Cartoon characters of cats.

I glance around for a litter box, a scratching post, or a bowl of Friskies; some sign of the animals. "Uh...I see no evidence about," I preface, timidly, "but, is there a cat living here?"

"Oh, that's Mr. Greeley. He only eats here. He's out somewhere."

"I see. Your father was like that, wasn't he— coming and going as he pleased?"

She looks down and sighs, acknowledging my perception. I have hit the mark.

Why do I receive two cartoon characters when asking about her parents? And each one, appearing and disappearing. Cartoons aren't real. How can someone's parents not be real?

"I'm adopted," she blurts out, before I have the chance to arrive at the answer.

Oh my God. I get it. Her parents are symbolized in my mind as cartoons, as a way of saying they're not real. *How clever.*

The Cheshire Cat appears to me again, and then disappears. "I never knew my real father," she adds. "And yes, my adopted father was always in and out of my life. He only went along with my adoption for my mother's sake."

"Your mother, Snagglepuss."

"What?"

"Nothing. Never mind." I look around the place some more. "You rent this whole house yourself?"

"Yep."

"It can't be cheap."

"It isn't."

"What do you do for work?"

"I work for a magazine publishing company."

"Good for you. You'll work for yourself before long."

She smiles. "I want to."

"You want to know why I see your mother as an angel?"

"Please."

"She gave you the gift of self-sufficiency, the ability to help yourself. If she didn't abandon you, maybe you wouldn't be so powerful in the world. Most people I know your age, especially here in Hawaii, are still living with their parents. The theme of abandonment and leadership is strong in your life."

"Are you talking about my real mother or my adoptive mother?"

"Why, did your adoptive mother abandon you too?"

"She threatened to put me back up for adoption when I was sixteen, so I ran away."

"Oh my God! How terrible!" I expect her to be in tears over this, but she just stares at me defiantly. This girl is tough. "What an incredible story that is," I say. "And even more it reinforces my point. Look, you can go on hating both your adoptive parents if you want to, but it isn't going to do you any good. It'll only frustrate you and make you bitter. So why don't you try cutting them some slack, even thanking them for helping to mold you into who you are today? In case you haven't noticed, people are not all cut from the same cloth. They didn't have the where-with-all to be mothers. And you, unfortunately, had to bear the brunt of that. Sometimes life sucks."

We sit in silence for a bit. I close my eyes.

A heart shows itself to me, in my mind—a heart with an arrow through it. "I want you to look for a symbol," I tell her. "It'll appear to you soon, if you look for it. It's a pierced heart. It *must* have an arrow going through it for it to be your symbol. And it will serve to— "

Hmm, what will this sign serve to do for her? "Uh...It'll guide you in some way," I continue. "It'll let you know you're on the right track." It's the best answer I can imagine.

After the reading, we walk out to my rental car in silence. The gravel on the driveway makes crunching sounds under our feet. I hope I served this girl well.

The Pacific Ocean is spread out before us. We stop and look out at the beauty of it. I say, "Lucky we live Hawaii, yeah?" It's a local expression, and grammatically incorrect. We smile, and nod.

"Listen," she says thoughtfully. "You mentioned me working for myself. I've wanted to start my own dating service. What do you think?"

"Dating service, huh?"

"Yeah."

"You ever heard of Cupid? The God of Love?"

"Sure."

"He carries a quiver of arrows. I told you, the heart had to have an arrow through it right? I think this is your pierced heart! Go for it!"

On the way to the airport I stop at a lunch counter and order a chicken plate. The place is part of an old house; everyone eats on a large porch. When my number is called I take my plate and sit down facing the ocean. God! Hawaii is gorgeous!

No silverware.

I get up, return to the counter and ask the girl, "Can I have some silverware?"

"Right over there," she says, pointing over to a small table on my left. I walk over to the table, and just above the silverware tray hangs a sign. It's a regular piece of office paper with a big heart drawn on it. A tack, used to post the paper on the wall, is pierced right through the heart.

Below the heart someone wrote, *"Help Yourself!"*

Lessons in Perception

June 1, 2004

Late Evening

The drone of the plane has a narcotic effect on me. But I can't sleep. I am anxious about this trip.

I've arranged to spend two months in New York City, swapping my Honolulu cottage for a Manhattan studio on East 14th Street. My accommodations are paid up, but otherwise, I only have $500 to my name. The success of this New York adventure depends on how many psychic readings I can book. I have only two so far. I have a long way to go if I am to live comfortably.

The plane is remarkably still, and quiet, save for the incessant drone of the engines. I am not only between sleep and awake, Hawaii and New York: I feel like I'm living my life somewhere between fact and fiction, too.

Occasionally, dream images briefly pop to mind: A man leaning back in an office chair with his feet up on a ridiculously tall desk. A snake with a gold key tucked securely in its coils. A barber, gingerly cutting hair.

I wake up with a sore neck, and shift position. A deep voice booms inside me, "You will have lessons in perception."

I open my eyes, and try to ascertain whether I really heard the voice in my head or not. I guess I *must* have heard it. "Lessons in perception," it said. Hmm.

The guy next to me is totally passed out. He's *been* out since dinner. How I wish I could sleep on a plane. I take in a few scenes from a Harry Potter movie. I like watching a movie with the sound off. You can concentrate on the acting and directing better that way.

A snake appears on the screen. It's safeguarding a key and hissing at a girl! She waves a wand and the snake turns into a clown.

I love this psychic mind! It's like magic. I've noticed this mental place I'm in—between sleep and awake—is conducive to retrieving psychic impressions. And they're always so symbolically rich.

A key opens doors. A snake is a healing symbol; it sheds its old skin. I fear snake, but am also intrigued by him. I fear change, but am intrigued by the new me that's emerging. This scene in the movie is about students learning magic. Maybe *I'm* learning magic. A shiver runs through me.

I stare down the cabin of the plane. What else is there to do? From my position, in the center aisle toward the rear of the plane, I can see eight television screens. Each one has a different hue. The two closest to me are kind of brown. Another one to the right is redder. Another, farther down, has a purple tint.

I examine them to determine which one is the most real looking. If I look at any one long enough I just accept it as normal reality. Without the perspective of the others, I couldn't tell—

Here it *is*! "Lessons in perception."

"What do you conclude from it?" Teacher asks.

"We all perceive differently? No two things are truly identical?

How do I know what is real? I am who I perceive myself to be, yet each person who sees me, sees me differently."

He offers no response. I add, "How about—All perceptions are valid?"

"Why does this matter to you right now? Why are you seeing this?"

"Is it that I need to accept different realities to open up psychically?"

"Could be."

This "could be" is all I am to hear on the subject. My guide is notoriously ambiguous, and this I understand. If I were ever to receive directives from him I would be highly suspicious. Our guides are just that, guides.

I have to go to the bathroom. Quietly, I unbuckle my safety belt, and slip my feet into my shoes. As I walk to the back of the plane, I scan the faces of the aft passengers. I don't recognize any of them from the terminal.

Near the galley, I take a moment to stretch my body, which has gotten tight from sitting in the chair.

In the bathroom, I aim a stream of pee for the center of the bowl, rest my head against the sloped plastic wall, and sigh. We humans have created such an amazing world. I'm peeing, 39,000 feet above earth!

Walking Through a Dream

June 26, 2004

Early Afternoon

I made two house calls this morning; one in Soho, the other on the Upper East Side. And now I'm lying in Central Park with lunch and a book! God, I could get used to this. I have one more reading this afternoon.

Every day I try to learn more about out what is happening in my mind when I'm performing a psychic reading.

My psychic mind seems indiscriminate in the selection of concepts it wants to show me, and my clients. It's my conscious analytical mind that sees implications in the visions I dream up. My conscious mind wants to see purpose and meaning in my psychic experiences.

It's my willingness to associate my fanciful thoughts with reality that facilitates my psychic awareness. If I imagine things with a mind that my imaginings will somehow be reflected in my reality—even if slightly differently—then, as I notice those correspondences, I'll begin to place more credence in my imagination.

I have to assume that those elements of my dreams that actually appear in my waking reality are calling me, *asking* to be recognized.

Late Afternoon

At the 72nd street subway station, I reflect on the challenging psychic reading I have just given to a woman in her thirties.

My vision of her future was not quite as glorified as the one she had set in her mind. What was coming through to me was that she needed to rethink some pretty major aspects of her life. She was, believe it or not, in a committed relationship with a gay man, trying to see him as her husband. He, she acknowledged, was behaving recklessly in his pursuit of sex outside of the relationship, and the implications I was seeing for her were not good.

I envisioned her single, but she feared being alone. Her resistance to leaving him left me depressed. Surely, I'll not see her again. Nor will I receive a referral from her. *God, I needed that referral!*

Still, I wasn't going to sugar coat the situation. I hope I served her well.

Getting off the train at 14th Street, I follow a current of people down an underground corridor smeared with a thin veneer of urine, skin cells, hair and spit. We, the people, shuffle along like sheep.

I approach an artist, drawing with colored pencils. Samples of his work are laid out on the floor around him. In one piece, a spaceship beams a mesmerizing light upon a circle of naive and uncertain people. I love it and imagine saying to my friends, as they admire it hanging in my Honolulu apartment, "Yeah, I picked it up from a subway artist in New York." But it's too late. The people have swept me away from him.

At the next platform I comment to myself how I feel like Dorothy from The Wizard of Oz, at that intersection on the yellow brick road, wondering which way to go.

A talented saxophonist, playing a Cole Porter song, seamlessly segues into Over the Rainbow. No wonder I was thinking of The Wizard of Oz. This melody never fails to draw out a longing from within me that I can barely describe, let alone satisfy. Within moments, I want to cry.

The song fills the station, the notes beautifully reverberating off the grungy tile. Everyone pretends to ignore it. The blank expressions worn by the majority of commuters are but masks.

I open my wallet, take out a dollar and throw it in the hat the artist has so prominently laid down before him. *There's a dream that I dreamed of once in a lullaby.*

I see no sign of a train, either from my left or my right. I must look lost, because a woman, who's been staring at me, asks (or demands, I'm not sure which), "Whey ya goin'?"

"Uh..."

"This side," she points, "is Brooklyn bound."

"Thanks."

Somewhere! Over the rainbow! Why take the train when I can walk home? It's not that far.

I climb the stairs to the street, walk a block, then cross an intersection. A man emerges from a clothing store, and sets off in my direction, walking a few feet behind me. He whistles a few notes of Over The Rainbow, and I burst out into a big smile.

He couldn't possibly have been in the train station, yet the song is in his head! I've got to be witnessing some kind of psychic telepathy here. What is it that causes the melody to leap like this, from one person to the next, even when they are beyond earshot of one another? The artist is reaching a wider audience than he thinks he's reaching.

I wonder if that painting of the spaceship will be there tomorrow?

Mr. Dreads Loves Me

July 15, 2004

Late Morning

God, it's a beautiful day in the East Village! I have no readings today, but that's okay; I've done twenty already. *Twenty*, from two, scheduled! They are referring their friends.

I'm daring to dream. I am glad not to be slaving away in that sweltering old ice cream plant.

At the corner of 1st and 1st, I stop and take a look around. Jesus, I'm on 1st and 1st—the "nexus of the city," as Jerry Seinfeld called it. I wonder if it's some kind of portal? It sure doesn't look it.

From my left, a huge dragonfly approaches and flies back and forth in front of me. I was raised in the country—I've seen lots of dragonflies. This ain't no ordinary dragonfly. It's a *Manhattan* dragonfly. Big, sparkling and electric green! It has to be the biggest dragonfly I've ever seen!

I read somewhere about dragonfly's symbolism. It represents magic and enlightenment.

Mentally, I say, "Hello!" It catches my eye and circles around me three times. Three is a number I associate with abundance and fertility. I have a sense that spirit is especially with me today.

My friend Bernard calls, suggesting I go to the TKTS booth in Times Square and get a late, half-price ticket to a Broadway show. "You have to choose from a limited list of shows," he says. "But if you can be spontaneous, you'll get a deal."

Early Evening

In Times Square, I glance down a side street and see the marquee for "I Am My Own Wife." Jefferson Mays won a Tony for his performance in this play. Hands down, it's the one I want to see.

Amazingly, I get a ticket.

Ten minutes before show time, I walk in to the theatre, and am ushered to one of the best seats in the house. I'm in the balcony, front-row center. If you drew an X through the theatre, either vertically or horizontally, my seat would be at the crux of it. I'm at the nexus of the theatre! "Thanks, Spirit!"

Mr. Mays is riveting to watch. He didn't win the Tony for nothing; he commandingly portrays nearly *forty* unique characters—women and men of various ages from Europe and America. He alone tells the story, which is quite captivating.

Charlotte von Mahlsdorf, a real-life transvestite whom Mays plays, was born into a culture at war. Charlotte's father, an abusive Nazi party leader, forced his son to join the Nazi Youth. At sixteen, after his mother fled the family, Charlotte killed his father by striking him over the head with a rolling pin.

You have to hate a guy pretty badly to kill him.

As I watched Mr. Mays, I thought of when I performed in The Laramie Project. I also played multiple characters. I would love to do that again, though lighter material would be nice. Somehow, I know I will perform in this way; playing multiple characters. This knowing is based solely on a sense that I'm looking at something familiar. Nothing more. But I'm willing to claim it, and do my part to make it happen. How exciting!

The story of how Charlotte survived her father, the war, and the years following it—especially as a transvestite—is unbelievable, tragic and compelling. Later in Charlotte's life, allegations surfaced that she had supplied information to the secret police in East Germany, and profited from the breakup of Jewish homes. Charlotte was both a sad and inspiring figure, who learned to do whatever she needed to survive. The audience is left wondering about the truth, confused as to whether to praise or revile her.

Evening

I leave the theatre in a swirl of incongruous emotions—about humanity, Mays' performance, and Charlotte. Awe, anger, pity, gratitude, and scorn, are all swirling within me. To my right, is Times Square, a throng of people. I can't handle people right now. I just want to crawl down an alley and be alone for a while.

I turn left, and walk a block and a half, to a quiet spot. Leaning against a tall, granite building, I stare down at the pavement in reflection. It rained while I was in the theatre. I worry about my ass getting wet. After what I've just seen, this thought makes me feel really petty.

The streets and buildings glisten from the rain. Everything is slightly steamy. Added to the usual din of the city is the hissing sound of water misting off the tires of passing cars.

A young man, of an uncertain character, in dread locks and a Snoop Dog T-shirt, wheels a cart of cleaning supplies directly towards me. He's not someone I want to have contact with right now. I sense he's taking an interest in me. *God, please don't talk to me.*

"Why on *earth*," he asks me in a loud voice, "are you standing there looking so serious? What are you thinking about?"

"I just saw a play, and it moved me."

The man scans the sidewalk for a moment, thinking about this. "The way," he says, dramatically, followed by a pause, "is already paved."

"I'm becoming aware of that," I reply, with confidence, even though I'm not at all sure I believe it. I've said it though. Maybe I really do believe the way is already paved.

The city has somehow become muted, as if we were in a film and the soundtrack was turned off. Time is moving through Jell-O. "I love you like a brother," he says, holding out his hand. His palm is pink, a network of train tracks, like a map of the subway.

My God! I reach out tentatively, and grasp his hand. Upon holding it, I look into his eyes and say, "I love you, too."

Is this happening?

The peculiar joy I feel, upon saying such obvious and liberating words to this stranger, has caught me off guard. My eyes are watering again.

"This is New York!" the guy shouts. I can't help smiling.

"That's right," he says. "A smile like that—you can do *anything* in New York!" With a twinkle in his eye, he points up to heaven and adds, "God told me to tell you that."

Dragonfly Medicine

July 16, 2004

Morning

"And with that, he moved on. I thought for sure he was going to ask me for money. Mom, I *floated* home. I don't think I've ever wanted to thank anyone so much. I'm telling you, it was like I met an angel."

"It sounds like it. You're having quite the experience there in New York."

"This *city*! It has a way of lifting you up. The couple I swapped apartments with—as it turns out, we have a lot in common..."

"How did you meet them again?"

"Through my friend, Laura. They're friends of hers. I can't remember exactly how all this got started. I think Laura sent out an email, saying her friends were looking to come to Hawaii for a while and, 'Did anyone want to go to New York in exchange?'. I mean, I never asked for it, but boy, it sure feels like it was meant to be. They have a book on symbols here in their living room that references the dragonfly. You know how a dragonfly hovers, and then seems to instantly disappear before your eyes? The author suggests a kind of magic is at hand, that those iridescent colors on their wings represent extraordinary experiences that don't happen everyday. I see the connection in my life, Ma. It's like the dragonfly really is communicating with me. Isn't it beautiful?"

"Yes. It sure is."

Early Afternoon
Walking along Central Park West, I hear an A train racing uptown through the grill in the sidewalk. Ella Fitzgerald sings in my mind, "Yaooooou must take the A traaainn tooo go to Sugar Hill way up in Harlem!"

This reminds me of a dream I had last night in which I was using a new, high tech communication system called Submail, something of a cross between email and subway transportation. I stood inside a tunnel that ran from New York to Paris. It was made of a glowing fiber-optic material. In the tunnel, an echo never faded. Even a thought would echo. I heard the word, "submail" come in from Paris. I knew it would travel past me, through space, undiminished, forever.

In my dream the system was very real and made absolute sense. I clearly saw that it would solve big societal problems. But now, from the perspective of reality, it sounds completely silly.

I continue my walk up Central Park West, nagged by the feeling that my dream was showing me something important about the future. Just ahead of me, a woman in her seventies stands on the edge of the sidewalk, holding a flower in her hand. She sings a song in French, in the hopes her entertainment will inspire people to give her money.

The trees above me chatter in the wind. They seem to be giggling over some joke. A uniformed man pushes a broom at the edge of the street. From behind me, a small voice cries,

"Mommy, what's he doing?" Mommy's sigh of exasperation blows through the trees. "What's it *look* like he's doing?" she replies. "He's sweeping the street."

"Why?"

I want to see this boy, and his mother, so I stop and let them pass me. As an excuse for my action, I feign interest in a squirrel that's frantically chewing on a nut, except the squirrel really does interest me because he eats his morsel as if it were the only food he'd come across in a week.

"Why, Mommy?"

"Because when the street gets dirty you have to clean it."

The squirrel suddenly could not be less interested in the nut. He abruptly discards his nutshell and moves on. I can hear the hard-drive in the little boy's head whirring as he saves the role of the street sweeper in his memory banks. He looks like me, when I was his age.

"Why does the street get dirty?"

He asks questions like I did, too. I still ask questions, constantly. To a large degree, psychic ability depends upon noticing details and stopping to ask questions.

"Because there are a lot of people, and that's what happens," the mother replies. As they walk past me, I turn to her and joke, "We're learning something new every day, huh?" She rolls her right eye at me, and turns a slight smile out of the corner of her mouth. It's a discreet little gesture, polite and obliging, yet sufficiently curt enough to convey to me she wants no further contact. She picks up the pace, pulling at the boy, in a demonstration of how to not talk to strangers.

As he's being dragged away, the boy's attention is fully fixed on me. I feel compelled to subliminally transmit a message to him. I smile and telepathically say, "How beautifully conscientious and aware you are! Use your gift to help your world be a more beautiful place. Exercise trust and you will have a rich life along with the wisdom of many wonderful experiences."

As if to let me know he hears me, he smiles slightly before turning away.

At the Museum of Natural History I buy a ticket to a show on space travel playing in the Rose Planetarium. As I lay back in my seat, a gorgeous pitch-black sky with countless, vibrant stars is presented on a domed ceiling. Within minutes, we are traveling in a space ship at intergalactic speed to the edge of what we know to be our universe. The size and scope of space is so breathtaking to experience I became emotionally overwhelmed.

Eventually, we reach an inconceivably distant point, and stop, to just float in the void for a bit. After a moment of silence, our narrator and planetary guide presents a hypothesis that we will one day find a wormhole, a portal in space and time, through which we can instantly return home.

The stars begin to warp into a spiral and in a flash we enter a tunnel. Lights stream past us at spectacular speed.

Hey! I recognize this, from past meditations! It's very similar to when I traveled into my psychic portal, the flower. It's the same kaleidoscope of colors.

Oh! I know what "submail" is! *Subliminal messages!*

Boy From OZ
July 17, 2004

Afternoon
Raymond, a tall, lanky Asian in his forties lives in a gorgeous two-story apartment with a roof top deck in Manhattan's Gramercy district. He slouches into his white leather sofa, clasps his hands together, and says, "I want to connect with my spirit guide. I've been seeing a psychic who's been working on this with me for two years now, but I haven't gotten anywhere. I try to meditate. But I just don't see anything. I don't hear anything. I don't feel any presence. This psychic keeps saying, 'Do you see anyone?' and I don't."

"Well, it sounds like you would benefit from a different approach. I think you know this but, to be clear, a connection to your guide won't come from a psychic. All anyone can do is help facilitate the process for you."

"I do know that."

"Okay. And your guide will communicate to you any way you will listen, any way you are willing to receive the information."

"You think I'm looking in the wrong place?"

"Maybe it's not happening in meditation. Let's say you've been trying to reach a friend. You keep dialing his home phone number to talk with him, but he never answers. Are you going to keep using the same method to reach him? No. You'll call his cell phone, try his office. You'll email, call his mother. If your guide is trying to reach you and you're not picking up the phone, so to speak, then he will reach out to you in other ways. The first lessons from your spirit guide are probably going to be about the nature of your communication. Subsequent lessons will usually be about faith in the process or trusting yourself."

"How do you know this?"

"These were my first lessons. They continue to be. It's a standard lesson plan. Your question is revealing, Raymond. It underscores you want proof for everything. What proof will satisfy you that your guide is active in your life, present with you? Have you thought about that?"

"I don't know."

"Well, this work requires we accept a different set of laws. The whole thing happens in your imagination. And this poses a dilemma as far as feeling anything 'real' goes. You've said this meditation approach you've been taking doesn't work. I believe it *can* work, but you're not letting it. You've defeated yourself, because you don't believe in your own ability to recognize your guide's presence. You've repeated it like an affirmation— 'I try, but I never see or feel anything.' You're setting yourself up for failure with these words." Raymond seems to take this in. He's staring at a clay pot on the coffee table.

I continue, "Say, for example, your mother came from another country and gave you up for adoption. Let's say that you were raised by someone other than your mother. Think of how it would be to meet your mother—a foreigner—for the first time, as an adult. You would have all these preconceived ideas about her, as to her appearance, her personality, customs, and talents. But then you would meet her, and many of those ideas would be totally out the window. You would have to come to a new acceptance as to who she is. And that would take time."

"That's so weird you say this. My mother lived in Singapore. She gave me to my grandmother when I was born. I was raised in Hong Kong and only met my mother later when I was in my teens."

I laugh. "Stuff we make up is often psychic. Pay attention to statements you make that start with, 'It's as if...' because they often end up being psychic visions."

As I listen to myself talking to Raymond, I'm surprised by how much I've learned along the way on this journey. I don't sound like the Derek I've ever known. Expressing these concepts helps me understand them. I'm beginning to feel like I've assimilated some of my guide's teachings into my life.

"In the film 'It's a Wonderful Life,' does George recognize Clarence as his Guardian Angel at first? No. And you probably won't recognize your guide at first either. Your guide is like a teacher. A teacher teaches you stuff you *don't know*.

"Lets play a game. We're not going to meditate, okay? We're just going to close our eyes."

"Okay."

"Can you picture a tree?"

"Yes," Raymond says.

"Great. What kind of tree is it?"

"It's a Willow tree."

"Okay. Interesting. That alone is symbolic." For a moment, I recall some research I did on the symbolism of trees. Willows metaphorically weep. They require a lot of water, which symbolizes emotions. I remember reading that before aspirin was invented, the bark of Willow trees was used to treat pain. I go out on a limb. "Raymond, did you take aspirin or Tylenol before I came over?"

Awkward pause. Raymond stares at me in disbelief. "You can tell I took Tylenol?"

"Late party last night?"

Raymond smiles. "I don't get how you know that."

"This is not the time to explain it. So you saw a Willow tree. See how easy this is? Forget about meditation. That's too intimidating. Now, picture someone you don't know, anyone, any age. Describe who you see."

"Uh... A boy, he's nine."

"Nine years old," I repeat. "Okay, what's he doing? Give me details."

"He's in a dining room with his family. He's eager to leave the table. Now he's looking and pointing out a big window."

"What does he want?"

"Even though he's young," Raymond says, "he wants to see the world."

"Do you get anything else?"

"No. That's all he's doing."

"Okay. This boy could be a guide, Raymond. Your guide could play different characters for you. He might do this to convey different messages. I want you to erase the image now, like a teacher erasing a blackboard. You're creating a blank slate. Now picture someone else. Who do you see?"

"I see a man. He's forty."

"You're getting specific ages. Anything specific is important. What else about him?"

"He's taking me to the beach," Raymond continues. "He's pointing across the ocean, like to a foreign land where he wants to go."

"Raymond, sometimes, when we're in our imagination like this, there are things we 'actually' see, like the man and the beach. And then there are things we have more of a 'knowing' about. Like the guy being forty for example—he's not wearing that on his chest. You simply know it. What else do you *know*, but don't *see*?"

"He's Australian. We're in Australia."

"Excellent. Try talking to him. What does he do for a living?"

"He isn't saying. He's just pointing, like I said." As Raymond is talking, I am also imagining his Australian guy on the beach. The Australian guy in *my* imagination does a quick cartwheel across the sand, and then winks at me.

I ask, "Does he want to show you anything else?"

"No."

"Okay, open your eyes. Raymond, your guide is communicating to you through these people. They may exist in your life or not. What you just briefly experienced in your imagination I call Symbolic Reality. The people, scenery and events that appear in this imaginary place in your mind have real meaning. The scenes may be simple, but they can guide you in surprising ways."

"But I'm just making all this up!" Raymond cries.

"No, you're not! That's what I'm trying to tell you! For example, are you planning a foreign trip?"

"I'm always planning a foreign trip."

"So the fact that this guy is pointing overseas is not meaningless."

"It just doesn't mean anything to me. What's he *saying*?"

"You're not recognizing valuable information when you see it, Raymond. Your guide is subtle and will give you more when you will listen. There's depth to this but you have to *look* for it. In meditative journeys such as this, the specific aspects of the journey are important. A nine-year-old boy. A forty-year-old Australian. The dining room table. The window. Pointing across the ocean. Note them and see how they correspond to your life. What was the boy looking out the window at again?"

"Just out, far away. To America, I suppose."

"And the Australian? He pointed out over the ocean. What country was he pointing to?"

"America also. Definitely."

"Okay, so what does America mean to you?"

"It's the land of opportunity."

"There you go. He could be saying you have opportunity coming, and it's here in America. Where were you born?"

"China."

"So maybe that nine year old boy was you, in a sense."

Raymond thinks for a moment, then says, "I had a friend who just died. He was Australian. And actually, he was forty. You think it was him?"

"Of course. I would explore that angle. Symbolic reality is multi-dimensional, Raymond. This takes a while to grasp, but the forty-year-old in your vision can be your friend *and* your guide. And maybe someone else too. One key to all this is remembering that these scenes haven't come to you for nothing; they came to you for a *reason*. Look to see or hear something that correlates to one of these images. It could be on television or as you're out and about...anywhere. When it happens, look around you and ask questions: 'What are the circumstances? Who are the players? What is the moral of this little scene?' Answering these questions will reveal messages from your spirit guide."

Early Evening

"Derek!" A familiar voice calls out from somewhere behind me. It's my friend Brent, who's also visiting New York, from Hawaii! We arranged to meet here to see a Broadway show, The Boy From Oz.

"Brent! Who knew we would be here in Times Square together?"

"I know, it's amazing, how our lives cross." As we give each other a long hug, the buildings around Times Square seem to sway with us a bit.

"If it weren't for the theatre, we might not have met, Brent. I remember first meeting you when I did Angels in America at Manoa Valley Theatre."

"The theatre has been like a backdrop for the story of our friendship, hasn't it?"

"It has. Pinch me, Brent! We're seeing Hugh Jackman tonight!"

"Are you as giggly about it as me?"

"We're going to walk in there like a couple of school girls going to a rock concert!" As we walk to the theatre, we catch up with each other. Brent asks, "So how are the readings going?"

"Amazing. I've read for like twenty five people while here in New York. One reading leads to the next. And how blessed I am, to spend the summer in the city like this! God, Brent, I could do readings from anywhere. The possibilities!"

"I'm jealous."

"Well, it sure beats scooping ice cream by hand, I'll tell you that! I'm happy again Brent! I'm starting to see that I can help people and travel at the same time. And, with my psychic reading business, I'll have the time to pursue acting!"

"That's so great."

"I see acting and psychic ability as related to each other, Brent. They both rely upon fully believing in the imagination."

"Interesting. I could see how that would be true. Sanford Meisner said acting was living truthfully under imaginary circumstances."

"Yes. Exactly." Changing the subject, I ask, "So how about you? What's going on?"

Through a big smile, Brent says, "Well, I'm thinking about applying to Columbia's acting program."

"Brent! That's terrific!"

"I have a lot to work out, but..."

"You'll work it out. *And* get accepted. I see it, Brent. We can live in New York together!" We arrive at the theatre and take our seats. Our eyes are wide open. The theatre is opulent, all red and gold. The audience is energized.

I say, "I don't know a thing about The Boy From Oz. Is it related to The Wizard of Oz?"

"No. I don't think so. Oz is Australia, I believe."

"Oh, right."

"It's about the life of Peter Allen, the entertainer," he adds. "Do you know who he was?"

"Don't think so. Before my time." We each sit in silence, pouring through the program. The lights go down, and the curtain opens to a small middle class family's kitchen. A boy, about nine years old, enters from our left, cartwheeling across the stage. He dances energetically about the kitchen, then makes his way over to a large window, out which he looks, wistfully. He talks to his mother of his dream to go to the big city. My neck begins to tingle. This is uncannily familiar.

Hugh Jackman enters with flair. He's electric! The women are swooning. The *men* are swooning! A woman, arriving to the show late, runs down the aisle to her seat. Jackman stops the show to make fun with her. "Decided to join us, darlin'?"

"I'm sorry," she calls out, "I couldn't get out of work!"

"Oh! What do you do?"

"I work in the news, in New Jersey. We had the Governor's scandal today, so..."

"Oh, of course. The Governor's scandal. We understand, completely." New Jersey's Governor was embarrassingly forced out of the closet today. Jackman adds, "These men with double lives!" He's cleverly referring to Peter Allen, Jackman's character, who lived a double life. Allen was married to Liza Minelli, but was gay. He straddled the sexual fence almost his whole life.

Playfully getting back into character, Jackman jumps on the piano, winks at us, and says, "Personally, I think the Governor's kinda sexy!" The audience roars. His energy and quick timing are incredible!

As he jumps onto the piano, I wonder, how old is Hugh Jackman? He's got a lot of stamina. I'd guess he's about forty. Just as I think this, a huge Australian flag descends from the ceiling. As Peter Allen, Jackman belts out a lyric about how he loves his country, but he is going to *New York City!*

Late Evening

Brent looks around the apartment I'm staying at on 14th Street and asks, "How did you find this place again?"

"I got it through a couple who know Laura. They wanted to go to Hawaii for the summer and were willing to swap their place. My mountain cottage was the perfect trade. And what was to prevent me from doing the swap? It's not like I have a job holding me back."

"Exactly. You know, more people should do this. What a great way to make travel more affordable."

"It sure beats a hotel," I say.

"So, let me get this straight, Derek. Your client today saw an Australian boy pointing out a window to America..."

"And I saw him do a cartwheel. No! That's not true. The forty-year-old did the cartwheel. And he winked at me, too, come to think of it. Just like Hugh Jackman did to the audience tonight. Anyway, isn't Hugh Jackman about forty?"

"I think so."

"God, Brent, it's just too much of a coincidence, don't you think, these parallels between my client's journey and tonight's show? The boy. The man. The ages. Australian. The window. The cartwheel. How can I not read into it? I'm turning forty. I also was married once, but am gay. I entertain on the stage. I crossed the ocean. The other direction, I admit, to go to Hawaii, but still."

"You *are* thinking about moving to New York."

"Yes, true. Maybe this is a sign. Maybe I will move to New York." We're silent for a minute. I say, "I told this guy, Raymond, 'Your spirit guide will talk to you any way you'll listen.' I said, 'Look for him to play different characters, to show up anywhere in your daily life.' And then I see tonight's show! It's like *his* spirit guide was sending a message to *me*. Or my guide was sending a message to me, through Raymond."

"That's a trip," Brent says.

"The more I study the psychic mind, the more I see how clever it is. And it's available. It's there, active in our lives every day. We go into other dimensions with our thoughts all the time, we just don't observe it."

My cell phone rings. "I'd say it's a sign, Derek," Brent replies.

I answer, "Hello?" Brent sips a wine and looks over some pictures on the wall.

"Hi, Derek, It's Joyce." Joyce is the theatre director at Hawaii Pacific University. Brent and I have each worked with her.

"Hey, Joyce! You'll never guess where I am, and who I'm with."

"Oh?"

"Brent, in New York. We just saw Hugh Jackman in The Boy From Oz."

"Oh, I hope it's not too late to call."

"No way! Are you kidding? We're still up, all amped."

"Well, this is great—I can kill two birds with one stone. I'm having auditions for Neil Simon's Broadway Bound later this month and I wanted to invite you to audition for the part of Stanley. And for Brent to come and play your brother!"

"Gosh, Joyce, thanks!" I would *love* to play Stanley. Turning to Brent I say, "She's inviting us to audition for Broadway Bound."

"Oh, I can't do that one," Brent says. "I committed to a show at The Actor's Group already."

"Bummer. Brent can't, Joyce. But I can if the auditions are the 30th or after?"

"The auditions *are* on the 30th."

"Great! I'll be there! Thanks for thinking of me, Joyce."

"Okay," she says. "I'll see you then. I'll let you guys go. Hi to Brent."

Hanging up, I say, "Joyce says, Hi."

Brent says to me, "Hi, Joyce," even though I've hung up already. Taking a seat on the couch he says, "Derek, did you think about the title of that play?"

"What about it?"

"Broadway Bound?"

"Oh my gosh. How could I have missed that? An added synchronicity." Brent's got the hang of this. "Guess I gotta move to New York, huh?"

"Yeah," he says, "And maybe you'll get that part, too."

Curiouser and Curiouser

RuPaul and The Mannequin

April 13, 2005

Afternoon

"You sure you wouldn't like some wine, Derek?"

"No, thanks."

My client is enjoying herself. She's invited three of her friends for an afternoon of psychic readings at her clothing boutique in Honolulu. Dresses, purses, jewelry, and shoes are all tastefully displayed. A little cheese tray has been laid out, along with some nuts and olives. It's a quiet Saturday and, though the store is open, no customers have come in. I have the sense she owns the business to outfit her friends more than anyone else.

For the last two hours, the women have listened in on each other's readings. I've kept the psychic insights light and fun. These women keep no secrets from one another; they've had fun watching me pick up on each other's personality traits.

After the last reading, one of the women asked, "Derek, how do you get your information?"

"I interpret information from my imagination. I let myself play, and go wherever my intuition guides me. Sometimes answers come from the walls or the things in the room. I'll allow the 'real' physical world around me to morph into an imaginary dreamscape. A kind of waking dream emerges, an alternate reality that I give the same credence as the conscious reality you and I know.

"For example, you see that gecko brooch there?" All eyes move to a colorful brooch made with rubies and other gemstones. "Gecko's have a definitive stare. When they look at you, they draw you into trance with one eye. Have you noticed how they do that? The next time a gecko stares at you, try mentally entering the eye to see what it is saying. This one says to me, 'I have a dream for you! I will share some of my talent with you!' I'm not quite sure what this means. Well, actually, maybe I do know. Lizards are the keepers of dreams. I think he's saying I will have a psychic dream. Maybe that he will come to me in a dream. Or that a dream of mine will have some correspondence in reality."

The ladies all stare at me blankly. *Derek, your example is too abstract. Not everyone understands your psychic language.*

"You have to think like a child to capture psychic insight. When you were all kids, you no doubt played with dolls. You briefly lived in an alternate reality. It was real to you. Well, if you were to ask a doll for psychic information, then carry on a conversation with that doll in your imagination, the doll would probably give you psychic information."

The ladies still gaze at me blankly.

I continue, "See this white mannequin over here with the oriental dress? In my imagination, she's raising her finger to me. She says, 'I have something to say!' Her voice is quite firm in my mind. She reminds me of that drag performing artist, Rupaul. Do you know her?" They all burst out laughing. They do know her. Rupaul is an actor, model, and songwriter, an iconic gender-bender, and race-bender. He's black, but performs as more of a blond white woman.

"It's funny," I say. "I know it makes no sense, and is strange, but you have to accept it regardless, and assume there's something psychic about it. She wants to say something to you, Arlette."

"Me?"

"I'll interpret what I see her saying and doing. She's flashing wide, white eyes. She is presenting herself to me as a black woman, but made up blonde, like she's trying to be white. She's standing on the coffee table, really confidently. She's wagging her finger at you, saying, "Girlfriend! Why are you letting your *so called* boyfriend run the show? If he's so *bad,* as you like to say, why don't you *leave him*?'"

The women all laugh. One says, "She has you pegged, Arlette."

"The psychic dreamscape is fun to explore. The characters we meet there are clever. Let's break the symbols down a bit. This model, or mannequin, appears African American to me. Why? To me, a black woman, as an archetype, represents strength and the quest for equality. That's why she's speaking to you about owning your power. Drag queens are another archetype. They live their lives on their own terms, nobody else's. They don't care what people think and often make decisions that defy social norms or conventions." I say this to Arlette as if it might apply to her.

She smiles knowingly back at me and says, “It’s so amazing, how that message applies to me.” The two other women exchange looks of disbelief. “I’ll say,” the owner of the store says, but apparently for a different reason. "This is so freaky, Derek."

"Why?" I ask.

"The other day, we painted that mannequin white. I didn't think that outfit looked right on her with her natural dark coloring. Underneath, she’s really a black mannequin."

Dreaming Lizard

August 17, 2005

Late Afternoon

Last night, I dreamed I was in a car with a woman, driving across a frozen tundra on a clear, dark night. I remarked at how flat the earth was—that it seemed to go on forever. She said, "The Northern Lights are dancing spectacularly this year. Only a few people have the ability to see them."

The lights in the sky became a huge cornucopia of orchids. This colorful bouquet of flowers then twisted into a tornado. For a while, it danced spectacularly in the distance and I watched the colors play with one another. Then as the tornado moved closer to us, it became ominous and threatening. "My God!" I screamed, "It's going to slam into us!"

Now, as I twirl my fingers in the sand at Ala Moana beach, I think about my dream. This morning, my boyfriend Ken made a centerpiece out of flowers for my kitchen table. He picked a few flowers off my Plumeria tree, and then arranged them with some orchids in a banana-split ice cream dish.

Elements of our dreams regularly appear in our subsequent waking reality. Dreams are like composite pictures, twisted visions of scenes from life. They seem to symbolically reflect our hopes and fears.

Dusk is nearing. A cluster of dark, blue-gray clouds floats just above the horizon. Higher up, I see a thin ribbon of orange swirled into some pink, cotton-candy-like clouds. All this is reflected below in the metallic water, which acts as a mirror.

From beyond the horizon, yellow sunlight majestically shoots upwards. I never saw the sky this yellow! High up, a bluer sky becomes paler and paler. Low down at the horizon, blue mixes with yellow, making a muddy green.

Here I am looking at a sky of colors, dynamically shifting. This is also just like my dream. Psychic perceptions clearly happen all the time. I see them most when I engage in a kind of matchmaking game, correlating "dream" images with "real" ones. When something calls my attention, because it feels vaguely familiar, I spend time with it, asking, where have I seen this before?

Since my dream is a composite picture of pieces from my waking reality, then my question is, why *these* pieces—orchids, sky, colors, etc? Orchids remind me of beauty, Hawaii. Cornucopia is bounty, abundance. A tornado represents awesome power—the power of the wind. It reminds me of my wolf guide.

Hmm. In the end, I'm always left wondering. There are so many ways to interpret symbols and dreams. I guess that means we're free to entertain different ways of looking at the dream experience. And our waking experience too!

I feel the need to talk with someone, so I pick up the phone and call my friend Jim. We performed together in a play called The Laramie Project. Of all my friends, Jim is the most psychic. We often talk about dreams.

"Lucky we live Hawaii, Jim."

"Hey, yeah! Where are you, Derek?"

"At Ala Moana, looking at one of the most beautiful sunsets you can imagine."

"I don't have to imagine it. I can see it myself, right out my window. What are you up to?"

"Nothing, actually. You?"

"It's my nephew's birthday tonight. You going out?"

"No, probably not, Jim. I thought of you because I dreamed of this sky I'm looking at."

"Funny you mention it. I had a dream about you last night."

"You did?"

"Derek, does a gecko mean anything to you?"

"Oh, my God! Yes, definitely. I recently had a gecko tell me something about sending a dream to me or having a dream come true. And actually, a dream of mine *has* come true! I'm looking at it. I dreamed of this colorful sky."

Jim says, "Well, in my dream, I was in the desert under a palm tree, and you came walking up to me. A gecko ran down the tree and the two of you danced like children around it."

"Jim! That is so psychic. You have no idea. Because the lizard told me he had a dream for me. Not only that, but I was talking to some clients about how I envision psychic insights. I was explaining how important I think it is to play like a child in that process. I think the lizard is validating that message."

"Wow, that's pretty cool."

"Jim, your dreams and thoughts are more psychic than you know. I'm starting to realize, people are sending psychic messages to each other *all the time.*"

Stormy Weather

August 20, 2005

Evening

A little plastic hula doll mechanically dances in the window to my right. Among the litter on the floor around me are spent incense sticks, wrinkled expense receipts, Chinese money envelopes, and a mousetrap. Outside, colored Christmas lights blink around a plastic figure of a fat woman gazing into a crystal ball. A neon light reads, "Fortune Teller."

As I look around at it all, I wonder, why do I do it? I do it because I need the money, and I'm gaining experience. Alec closed Karma Cat, so I started doing readings at this tacky psychic shop in Waikiki. Here, I can meet people with a diverse range of problems who come from all over the country. I'm just moonlighting though. Hopefully it won't be for long.

My client is a big girl, with big, blond hair, and a face covered in lots of makeup. Like most of the clients here, she's a tourist. "When I get back home, I need to find a new job," she says. "I'm wondering if you can tell me about it." I flip two tarot cards from a deck called Motherpeace, created by Karen Vogel and Vicky Noble. The cards are Daughter of Swords, and Tower of Destruction. The Daughter card features a young woman blowing wind with a tornado behind her. The Daughter card is sometimes called a Page. Pages deliver messages. Placed as it is, next to the Tower of Destruction, I take the Daughter of Swords to mean, news of an upset, in this case, a storm.

"Storm's coming," I tell her.

The woman gives me a cursory nod then leans forward impatiently, if to say, yeah, yeah, now tell me about the job. I continue, "I know you think this is irrelevant information, but it's not to me. This one's a doozie. It apparently interferes with your job hunt in a big way. How long have you been looking?"

"About a month."

I decide to look at the situation clairvoyantly. Lately, I've been drawn to see what psychic insights I can find in my own imagination. This is a conscious decision on my part. Psychic insights can't come to me unless I focus my attention on my imagination and look for them.

As soon as I close my eyes, in my mind I'm standing just outside a pair of sliding glass doors on a recreation deck, which extends off of the back of a house. I see some outdoor furniture, a gas grill, and some plants.

"You work out of your home?"

"No."

"Well," I continue, "regarding your work, when I look at the situation clairvoyantly, with my mind's eye, I'm brought to the porch of a house." In my imagination, I walk to the edge of the porch and look out. There's water immediately beneath me. I could dive right in, except it's really dirty. Disgusting actually. Oil, dead fish and all kinds of trash are in it.

"You live on the water?"

"No."

"Where do you live?"

"New Orleans."

Working Blind

August 30, 2005

Late Morning

Performing a reading is like walking in the dark. All a psychic has is his or her imagination. And the conscious mind doesn't consider the imagination to be a reliable place to establish facts.

A client comes asking about a situation, and sometimes—as in the case with this woman from New Orleans—I see something that seems totally unrelated to her experience. The accuracy of my psychic visions is dependent upon my client's willingness to associate what I see with what is ultimately experienced.

When I entertain thoughts that I've designed to be telepathic, I have to operate under the premise that everything happens for a reason. If I dismiss an idea I have as irrelevant, I might be missing a message. Perhaps psychic insights are purely symbolic or figurative. And only sometimes are they real. Actually, I'm not sure what is real anymore.

Hurricane Katrina has flattened New Orleans. Now I understand why I envisioned the oily water beneath my client's deck. I remember feeling that the house was like a boat on the water. Since she didn't have any connection to what I was saying at the time, I took the whole vision figuratively. I had no choice.

The storm symbolized a major event to me. The poisoned environment meant the location wasn't right or that the atmosphere was not conducive for her result. I remember telling her I didn't think she was living in the area in which her job would ultimately be located. I told her I saw her moving north, maybe to another state, living in a different house: a house in which she would work. I saw a man doing renovation work on the place. As I saw it, she'd only have to work part time because of him. She confirmed she was dating a guy in construction, but the rest of my vision seemed unlikely to her.

I tried to paint a happy picture for her, because she had a lot of anxiety over finding a job and my initial vision wasn't exactly reassuring. I saw her new house as having a yard. I saw a pine tree out back with a bird feeder hanging on it. I hope she's able to experience this vision. I only remember her scratching her head as she walked out of the psychic shop.

A Fruitful Tree

November 28, 2005

Early Afternoon

Meditation is like sex. Sometimes it's good and there's a connection, sometimes not. While meditating, I expend no effort to making anything happen. In the journeys where I felt most connected, I was never asking, "Am I there yet?" as if there is a destination. I'm learning to simply observe my experience. The journey is the destination.

Whatever happens in meditation must be happening for a reason. I'm still learning to accept what comes regardless of how I feel about it. Every time I seek an answer to a question, I get symbolic pictures or enigmatic concepts that raise even more questions! I think the process is mysterious like this by design, perhaps to arouse our curiosity.

Today, as I sink into meditation, I am aware of a powerful presence within me, which, at first, I cannot identify. Exploring the essence of it, I discover that I'm a tree; a giant white pine. Trees and rocks have been reliable instruments to help me get grounded. When I imagine becoming them, my body becomes still more easily.

For a while, I bask in the experience of being the tree, the trunk, the huge sagging limbs, and the prickly green needles. My body has completely changed according to my consciousness. The presence within me says, "Your blood is now water and sap." I feel myself to be a mature tree. "You are part of a great forest canopy," the presence explains. As I look down, I see many younger trees on the forest floor, some fifty feet below me. "See how you protect the saplings below?"

As soon as I become aware of this, a kind of energetic orb is held out in front of me. It's translucent, purple. White strands of dynamic electricity radiate from its center. Every time I look at it, it disappears. I can only catch glimpses of it. I seem to see it best with my peripheral vision. Like when I look at a star—it appears in sharper focus when I look just to the side of it.

The orb becomes a collection of little pulp sacs each turning inside itself. It reminds me of a cluster of grapes, all squished together. It is alive with movement. I let it mesmerize me.

In my meditations, I routinely look for the object that will put me into trance. This object is my portal to the psychic realm of Symbolic Reality. As I gaze into this purple ball, I feel myself becoming absorbed into it. And that I am turned inside out.

"Yes!" the Presence says, "Don't *look* at it. *Become* it!"

I *am* the cluster now. I have decided to become it. I am the thick, purple fluid of grape juice, nutritionally powerful and dense. I am impenetrable, and there is great potential in me. "I'm working in color," an unfamiliar female voice says to me. "I'm especially interested in the vibrational healing quality of the color purple for you."

Lightning flashes. Telepathically, she tells me it's spiritual electricity. I'm not sure what that means. But I know I'm not the flesh of this organism anymore. I am its seed. I ask, I am a grape *seed?*

"Yes," the woman says, in reply. It's as if I were playing charades with someone and finally guessed the clues right. Then she says, "A supplement at the health food store."

Late Afternoon

The health food store closest to me is called Huckleberry Farms. It's not until I pull up to the place that it occurs to me that the store's name is related to the concentrated berry I became in my meditation. As I open the door and step inside, I wonder, what *is* a huckleberry exactly? Could that have been what I was seeing?

The store is clean and well lit, with wood floors and a neutral scent. A young woman stands behind a cash register set up on an island counter. Another woman browses the supplement isle. I ask the clerk, "Do you carry a grape seed extract or know what something like that would be used for?"

Out of the corner of my eye I see the woman browsing the supplements turn to me. The clerk says, "We have Grape*fruit* Seed Extract."

"No," I reply. "Not grapefruit. Grape Seed." The clerk furrows her eyebrows, turns on her heel, and scans a wall of bottles nearby. One shelf displays a line of supplements featuring simply designed white labels with black text. Many of the names look scientific. I might as well be looking at a poster of the periodic table of the elements. The clerk takes one of these bottles off the shelf and says, "Maybe this." The label reads, "Masqueliers TRU-OPCs."

"What is it?" I ask, turning it in my hand to read the fine print on the back. Before she can answer, my eye falls upon a hint. Near the bottom of the label, I read, "from grape seeds", and then "antioxidant".

In the last few days, my sinuses have been acting up. I've wondered a few times if I've been getting enough immune system support. Maybe that woman from my meditation was suggesting this stuff can help me.

The clerk walks away. After a moment, the female customer turns to me. I can tell she wants to share some personal experience with me, but doesn't want to intrude on a stranger.

I look up at her and smile invitingly. "You can take this," she says to me, retrieving a bottle next to the grape seed stuff. "It's much better." She hands it to me. The label reads "Pycnogenol."

"My husband's been taking it and it's amazing."

"Is this the same stuff as this?" I ask, comparing it with the bottle the clerk showed me. "Because I was told to look for grape seeds." I hope she doesn't ask me who made this recommendation. I would feel silly saying, "A lady I heard while I was in a trance." She'd think I was nuts.

"They're both antioxidants," the customer says. "They perform the same function." She takes the bottle back from me, turns it over and squints, reading it. "Let's see...that's right," she says, pointing to the small print on the label. "This is extract of a pine tree."

"A pine tree?" The tree from my meditation! "Really, that's...amazing." I don't know what to do. Here I have the essence of pine trees in one hand and the essence of grapes in the other. Both were shown to me. Which product is right?

I turn to ask the customer, but she's disappeared. She must have gone down one of the other aisles. The clerk is gone too, perhaps to an office or storeroom. Barry Manilow croons above me through speakers in the ceiling. *"Can't smile without you..."* He isn't any help. I tune in to Teacher, my guide. "So which one do I take?"

"It's your decision. Guides lead, remember? We don't tell you what to do."

"So one of these isn't wrong for me?"

No answer. Looking at the price, I see there is no way I can afford both of these products. I decide on the pine tree extract. Maybe I'll get the other one another time.

An Elusive Guide—Hummingbird

January 13, 2006

Early Evening

My client is chubby and cute, with soft, round Asian-American eyes. At the moment, she's desperate because her boyfriend broke up with her. She gives me a pleading look and asks, "Can I get him back?"

'Can I get him back?' is a common question in psychic readings. More often than not, the answer is 'no'. I hate disappointing a client. I want to tell the story as I see it, not lie to sugarcoat the situation.

I have no idea how I know why her relationship's over. I just do. It's a feeling more than anything. Sadness has come over me. I need a silver lining for this dark cloud, but first I have to help her with why the whole thing fell apart and how to move on.

The tape recorder softly whirs as I feel out an answer. My eyes move to a box of facial tissues propped on the sill. I've learned to keep the tissues handy. The tears can flow at any minute.

The tissue box has a fuzzy, pale blue aura around it, visible only to my third eye. I stall for time, trying to figure out how to approach saying this. She presses me, asking, "How do you see him? Can you see how he feels about me?"

A hummingbird and some flowers are printed on the tissue box. To my mind's eye, the hummingbird is alive, buzzing from flower to flower. The vision is enhanced by the whirring of the tape recorder, which sounds similar to the beating of the hummingbird's wings.

You can't get close to hummingbirds. They're skittish. "I'm sensing you think that if you tell him you want him back, it will scare him, and push him farther away." This seems like stating the obvious, but I say it anyway so she can hear it from someone other than herself—and probably her friends. "We don't always like what our intuition tells us."

Her shoulders drop in disappointment.

The hummingbird tries to get my attention again, this time by tugging at my shirtsleeve like a kid. He says to me, "Daddy, Daddy! Look at me!" Then he's back to the flowers.

I tell my client, "He's not ready to settle down yet. He's young or immature to me, still flitting from flower to flower." She indicates agreement with this statement, so I continue, letting the metaphor of flowers as women guide me. "I think there's someone else."

"He told me he wanted to go back to his ex."

"Mmm. So, there you go." The hummingbird works feverishly at another flower. "He keeps himself pretty busy, huh? Is one of your complaints that he doesn't make time for you?"

"Yes. He's always at work," she says. The hummingbird moves back to the original flower.

I ask, "Do you think there's more than one ex?"

"Is that what you see?"

Damn. Pandora's box. "It's possible," I tell her. "I can't be sure."

"Well, he has a son who takes up a lot of his time."

Oh! The hummingbird is his *kid*!? Maybe the hummingbird is role-playing both of them. "I *do* see the kid," I say. I wish I mentioned that before my client did. The hummingbird gave me the information and I didn't take it!

I hold her hand and continue talking with her. She takes a tissue, and the hummingbird zips off. At the end of her reading, I attempt to tie everything up with a nice bow. "Let time tell. It's hard to let go, but you will, and you'll be happy again. For now, your guy remains elusive. Sorry." My statements seem like platitudes.

"What's elusive?"

"You mean, what does it mean?"

"Yeah."

"Uh...like a hummingbird, you can't touch it. It always stays out of reach."

Mid-Evening

I order Chicken Katsu at a local diner, and take a seat in a plastic orange booth. As I wait for my dinner, I begin reading the script for a play I'm to perform in called Enchanted April.

Two pages into it, one of the characters, Lotty, laments, "My husband says that my mind is like a hummingbird. One never sees it land."

How strange. Here is reference to another hummingbird. I wonder if the hummingbird resonated with me because I was psychically seeing this moment: me reading about a hummingbird from this play? Perhaps the hummingbird is an active symbol, visiting me, as if I were a flower.

I feel reassured somehow, coming across a hummingbird right after my reading like this. It feels like a confirmation of the symbol's intelligence. I'm amazed at how often psychic insights can be gleaned from my surroundings.

It seems that if I design that a psychic symbol be present in my surroundings, then it *will be* in my surroundings. Initially, I may not consciously know what that psychic symbol is, but it *is* there. It's just up to me to perceive it. The moment I entertain a prospective psychic symbol, I will only *sense* its metaphorical value. Its appearance in my future will serve to confirm that value. But is the symbol's appearance then by chance? Or design?

Flowers, and the Mysterious Frenchman

February 19, 2006

Early Afternoon

I am lucky to work out of my home! I'm blessed to have a perfect little den for doing psychic readings. I am clinging on to my cottage on the mountain of course. Every time I imagine myself in Manhattan, I fear of living in a shoebox. Spirit, please help Ken and me find a special and convenient place to live in New York.

"You have such a great house," my client remarks, as she steps out my front door and onto my lanai. Maria has super straight, long, black hair that goes right to her knees. She must've been growing it for years.

"Everyone says that," I reply. "I am hesitant to give it up. I am hoping to move to Manhattan."

"I heard! You'll find a great place, I'm sure. You can do anything, Derek."

"Thanks for the vote of confidence!"

"Thank *you*, for the reading. I feel so much better. You're amazing!"

"Thanks," I smile, wondering what I possibly could have said to make her feel this way. My friend Richard has told me time and again, "Your words mean far more to the client than they do to you." I'm slowly learning that that must be true.

"Oh! Before I go," she says, pulling a picture out of her purse, "can I ask you to look at this photograph? Do you see something in this?"

Standing beside me, she holds up a photograph of a backyard flower garden. Behind the garden there's a tall brown fence made of wide wooden slats. The sun shines through the branches of a nearby tree in such a way that a pattern is created on the fence. It's not hard to see a face formed by the sun's light, and the tree's shadows.

"There's a face on the wall," I say.

"So you see it too! My mother says it's a spirit. I say it's a man. Which do you think it is?"

Here is an either/or question. But in the psychic world of symbolic reality, there is no either/or. To see things as either/or, this or that, is a classic indicator of conscious mind thinking. Psychic, intuitive thought is inclusive and limitless by nature.

"I actually have first hand experience about this question," I tell her. "My Spirit Guide has talked with me about this. Why can't it be a man *and* a spirit? The way I see it, he represents a real man and a spirit. I'll give you my observations and then we can see where it leads us, okay?"

"Okay."

"This is a man who tended flowers. He's obviously looking over this garden. I see a mustache on him, and a beret, with an emblem on it. Do you see all that?"

"Yeah, I do," she says, peering intently into the picture. The beret especially is so obvious. Amazing how the light does that.

"Do you know of a family relative or friend who was French and/or served in the army?" As I ask this of Maria, I think to myself—A man who tends flowers, and goes into the army—he had to be gay.

She thinks for a moment, says nothing. I ask, "Whose garden is this?"

"My mother's."

"He may be your mother's uncle or a relative of hers. But he definitely tended flowers," I tell her. Looking at the face again, I see it shift into two different expressions, like a holographic image. "He led a double life. Gay, but married, or at least hid his homosexuality from his family."

"Well my mother's brother did own a florist shop, and he died."

"*Really,*" I say, imbuing the word with deep mystery and knowing, as if she was sharing serious gossip.

"But I'll never tell her that part about him being gay," she adds. "She couldn't accept it."

"That's too bad. It's only speculation at this point anyway. She had a good relationship with him, did she?"

"Yeah, as far as I know."

"Let me ask you, do you believe the story I'm telling you? Does it sound reasonable?"

"Yes, I do. And I'll ask my mother, but why is he in this picture? What does he want?"

"He doesn't have to want anything. He loves flowers and hangs out with them. Then again, he may want to connect, resolve past conflicts. I get the sense he whispers into her ear as she's tending to the garden. He loves her. Why don't you tell her of my impressions? That way the door is open for more communication."

Maria leaves. A guy named Philip comes by. I recognize him as soon as he approaches the door. I did a reading for him about a year ago. For the life of me, I can't remember any of it.

I'm delighted to see clients return. It confirms I'm doing something right! "Come on in, Philip," I say, feeling a bit like a wolf as I lead him to my reading den.

It's rare for men to come see me. Ninety percent of my clients are women. Does he live on an outer island? What was his problem? I remember feeling frustrated by his story. He has to get past a mental block of some kind.

"I have it in my head you live on one of the outer islands, Philip."

"No, I vacation here with my family every year. I'm from California."

"Oh, right."

As soon as he plops into the chair, Philip cries, "My wife is asking me questions about my lover. I don't want to destroy my marriage, Derek. But I can't hide anymore, either." It's all coming back to me now. Philip is gay.

Philip truly loves his wife. He has managed to straddle two identities his whole life. He's genuinely torn. He desperately wants to preserve both his marriage and his homosexual identity.

Déjà vu is washing over me. "Philip," I ask, "Don't you own a flower shop?"

"Yeah. I want to talk to you about that too."

Oh my God. What does all this *mean*? Is it a symbolic confirmation of my last message? Or simply my psychic mind looping through time again? Maybe all that stuff I sensed for Maria was bogus.

No. It could have fit for her, too. "And you're not French by any chance, are you Philip?"

"I'm half French, yes. Why?"

"I just wondered." Yes, I really do wonder...

Evening

Tonight is the last night I will portray Antony Wilding, the wealthy, ladies' man in Matthew Barber's theatrical adaptation of the book Enchanted April. What a great escape it's been to enter Mr. Wilding's rich world! I'll feel sad to say goodbye to him.

As Antony, I am in my London flat, busy serving tea to two ladies. They have come calling in answer to an advertisement I posted seeking a summer tenant for my Italian villa.

I hand the two ladies, Lotty and Rose, a bunch of photographs that I took of the villa. The audience can't see our pictures. They're a bunch of old prop photographs the theatre had hanging around. Every night, the photos that the two actresses and I actually look at, change.

"Mr. Wilding," Rose calls out, sliding up to me with one of the photographs. "What's this?"

As it is written in the play, the picture Rose refers to is supposed to be of Mr. Wilding's thumb—the result of a slip with the camera as I took the picture. But what Laura (the woman playing Rose) and I are actually looking at is an old, black and white photograph of a man standing before a tree-shaded fence trimmed by a flower garden.

What a remarkable replay of events! I'm stupefied.

Jesus, how much time has passed? *Say your line Derek!* "That, I'm afraid," I say, with a bit too much of a pause, "is a picture of my thumb."

Something About an Actor

March 4, 2006

Early Afternoon

I'm having lunch with my friend John at the courtyard cafe in the Honolulu Academy of Arts. John is a handsome guy with a deep throaty voice. He's a writer, and a fellow student of oracles. While I'm partial to the Tarot, John takes to a Chinese divination system called the I Ching. He also teaches dream analysis.

"I had a dream a few nights ago," I tell him, "in which I was acting opposite Meryl Streep. I was either Tom Hanks or Robin Williams. I tried to see which one of them I was, but I couldn't find a mirror in which to see myself. A mirror would offer me definitive proof of my identity.

"I thought, since there is no mirror, if I could just step outside my body, then I could see myself, for who I really am.

"I was able to leave my body.

"And at this point, I was surprised to discover that I was nether Tom Hanks *nor* Robin Williams. I was an unknown actor. I felt indifferent about this."

As John pokes at his salad, I gaze at a water fountain in the courtyard. "I hope I don't end up an unknown actor, John."

"Derek, in my dream class, I encourage students who remember a dream to ask themselves if they were the 'I' in the dream, as in 'I'," he says, pointing to himself, "or the 'eye' as in, E-Y-E." He points to his eye. "In other words, are you playing observer or participant? Audience or actor? The perspective the dream mind takes can lend some meaning on its own."

"Hmm...I'll have to look at that. Now I'm thinking...Yesterday I read for a woman who wanted to know why her boyfriend's ex-girlfriend has been hanging around. In order to access what the ex-girlfriend's motivations might be, I pretended to enter the ex-girlfriend's mind in my imagination."

"That sounds scary. What'd you find?"

"That she was trying to smooth out the drama of their breakup," I reply. "I think she wants to be neutral in her former boyfriend's eyes, for him to see her more positively."

"She's a stalker."

"Basically. But John, the thing is, when I performed the imaginary exercise of looking out at the world through her eyes, I saw the boyfriend as standing by a red truck. So I asked my client if he had one, and it turns out he did."

"Wow, that's cool."

"John, I think my dream about playing the actor stepping outside of my body gave me the idea for this psychic technique. More and more I'm dreaming my future. It's as if I'm reliving facets of my dreams."

"Like constant déjà vu."

"Exactly. Over the past year, I've had a lot of dreams about film. Actors and teachers are always showing up. There's been a collective theme about teaching and performing. Finally, I assembled it into a message that I was to teach a psychic development class."

"You're teaching a class now?"

"It's been a big leap for me," I tell him. "But I talked with some clients about it, and they expressed interest. So I spent a few weeks coming up with some playful imagination exercises, and the next thing I know I've got a weekly class going with about ten students in it!"

"Good for you, Derek!"

"I'm pretty excited about it. Oh! My dream. There's another psychic part to it."

"Okay, go on."

"So in the dream, a teacher gave me an assignment to play my female self, and my male self, as separate characters in a one-man show. The script for this show turned out to be locked in a drawer, so I asked a theater manager for the key to unlock it. But he said the drawer containing my script was *never* locked."

"Will I be seeing you performing in drag?" John asks.

"If offered a role, I probably wouldn't say no! But anyway...I hold my psychic workshop in one of the classrooms at Unity Church. Yesterday, Saturday, I forgot my key to the classroom door, so I had to hunt down a janitor to get the room open. Once we got to the door, he pointed out that the room was already unlocked. It was very much like my dream, except the drawer in this case was a room. On Friday, if you can believe this, I got an opportunity to audition for two small day-player parts on the TV show Lost."

"Wow. That could be big for you."

"Well, I'm not holding my breath. I've been in that casting office before, and they haven't selected me yet. At least I'm getting called back.

"But my point is, the casting director told me I could play either Peter or Arthur. So here is this idea of playing *two roles*. I'm noticing components of my dreams are appearing in my waking reality. The characters might change, or the context might be different, but there are undeniably correlations to be made."

"Seems like your dream mind is tuned into the psychic channel, Derek."

"Tell me about it! I can't turn it off!"

Small Monkey

April 8th 2006

Early Morning

I feel sad this morning as I lie in bed. I'm not sure why. It's a beautiful day, and nothing is terribly wrong in my life. Maybe it was a dream I had. I curl back into the fetal position I was in upon waking, because I've learned that returning to the position I woke up in helps me remember my dreams.

I ask myself, "Where was I?" as if I'd been talking, and suddenly lost my train of thought. I can't remember anything, so I start thinking about the elements; earth, metal, air, fire, water. Water! Water feels familiar, so I consider some of its forms. Ocean, lake, river, tears. Tears! Yes, I remember now. I was crying! The whole dream was just me sobbing.

I wonder if this means some bad news will come to me. With some apprehension I record my dream in my dream journal. I'm trying to track if certain types of dreams are more likely to appear in my waking reality than others. I would think that realistic dreams—where the laws of physics aren't being bent—might be more psychic than surreal dreams. But I've noticed individual elements of surreal dreams can also be psychic.

At my kitchen table, I take the saucer from underneath my coffee cup and use it as a guide to help me draw a circle on a blank page in my psychic journal. It's part of a psychic exercise I plan on teaching to students of my psychic development class later this morning.

The idea is to draw within the circle, randomly, *without a plan to draw anything*. From this drawing, a psychic symbol comes. The crucial trick is to let the pencil lead me, not the other way around. As the pencil is moving across the page, I'll have no conscious knowledge of what it is drawing or why it is drawing it. To help facilitate this, I imagine my pencil as a character—a person I don't know, but might meet. I've learned that imagining the pencil as a character distracts my mind from planning something to draw. Planning is a function of the conscious mind. I want to tap into the psychic mind.

The person I imagine as the pencil is wearing a military or police uniform. Instantly, I feel him to be an authority. He barks an order at me as if I were in boot camp. "Cry me a river, Calibre! I want you to form a line, ya hear me!? Form a line! Left! Right! Left! Right!"

I know this is all quite silly, but psychic visions often are! So as bizarre as this is, I follow the official's instructions, drawing a line from left to right within the circle. As I do this, he says, "Lift up! Lift up!" And per his instructions, I make the line bend upwards. "Now again! Left! Right! Left! Right!" I return my pencil to the same point on the left side of the circle and again draw across. The man in uniform yells, "Fall down! Fall down!" My pencil turns down to the lower right.

I ask, "Now what?" The military official has disappeared from my imagination. "Hey!" I call out, "Come back. Tell me what I'm drawing."

The military official returns to my mind, except now his uniform has changed to a top hat and tails. He carries a cane and dances across the stage singing a line from a Cole Porter tune. "Don't fence me in! Don't fence me in!" Between the two lines I draw the lines of a fence.

I don't know why I've done this, *and that's the point*. Whatever comes, comes. I must have drawn it for a reason though. And that's what I want to find out. My abstract picture reminds me of a few things. Below my drawing, I list them.

The Eiffel Tower – On Its Side, A Pointy Bra Madonna Once Wore, A Stretched Stocking, Some Kind of Pulley System.

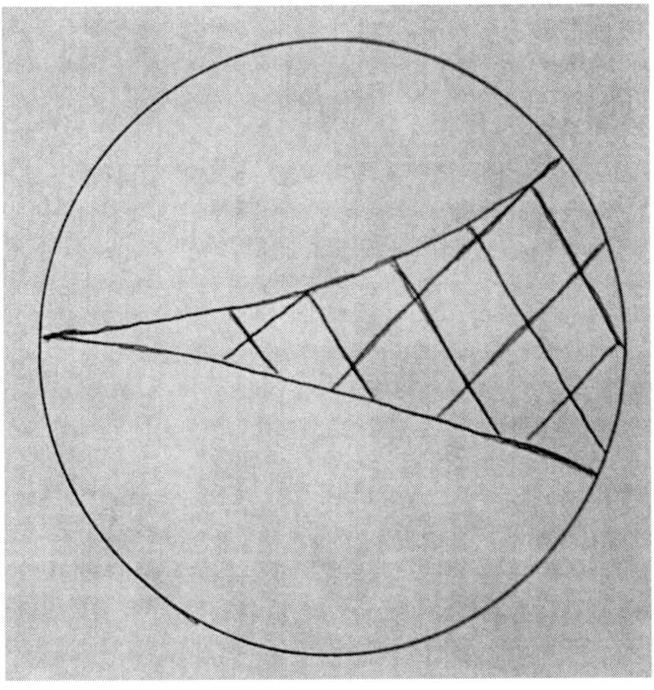

Mid-Morning

Nine women show up for my psychic class. The one man who was coming seems to have dropped out. I sense my class is too weird for him.

One of the students, Maile, reminds the rest of the group of a psychic vision she'd had while performing the circle drawing exercise the week prior. At the time, she drew what she interpreted to be a single red balloon among a bunch of other white balloons. We all indicate remembering her impression.

"Well," she continues, "This week I was reading a children's book, Curious George, to my daughter. I flipped the page and, to my amazement, there was a picture of these balloons; all plain, except one among them that was red!"

"Maile, that's wonderful," I say. "What a great psychic impression! Let me point out something I'm seeing in this. In our first class, I talked about how psychic ability is largely about being open and paying attention. Curiosity, you will remember, was one of the first words I wrote on the blackboard, as I listed qualities you must cultivate to awaken to your psychic ability. So to me, these balloons from *Curious* George are a really clever wink from Spirit.

"For you, this psychic impression also points to your daughter, perhaps underscoring the importance of cultivating *her* sense of curiosity. This balloon image is basically about one thing being singled out among others. I believe this to be a psychic vision of you or your daughter being chosen among a group, Maile."

"Oh Good! I've applied for her to go to a private school. I'm waiting to hear if she will be accepted."

"With each psychic impression you collect from class," I continue, "you're looking for a corresponding event to occur in your life. It's like the card game, Concentration. You're looking for two symbols, or concepts, that match. When Maile drew her balloon drawing last week, it was like drawing the first card of two cards that will eventually match. She remembers that first card. As she goes through her waking life, something happens that corresponds to that initial drawing.

"Let me give you another example. Last week I mentioned that my guide, the wolf, came to me in meditation and said, 'I want to take you to the forest.' Do you all remember me telling you that?" They all indicate that they remember. "At the time, I felt he was reminding me of the forest as a meditation sanctuary, and I think he was. But later that day I received an audition notice from Diamond Head Theatre for the musical "Into the Woods." As it turns out, one of the characters in this musical is *a wolf.* I thought, 'Ah ha! Wolf! Woods! I'll audition for it.

"But the next day, there is another audition for an A.R. Gurney play called "Sylvia" at The Actor's Group. It's about a guy going through a mid-life crisis who brings home a stray dog, much to the chagrin of his wife. It was originally written for Sarah Jessica Parker, who played the dog on Broadway.

"I thought, 'A dog is a kind of wolf,' so I went to that audition. I arrived early to read through the script a little. The play is hilarious. On Page 11, the character of the wife, who hates the dog, laments, 'Sylvia! What a name for a dog.'

"And the husband replies, 'No, it fits. I looked it up. It means, *She of the Woods.*'"

My students all smile. One of them asks, "Which play are you going to do? You have to get one of them!"

"Well, as it happens, the director of Sylvia called me and offered me a part in that play. I should say *parts*, actually, because in this show, one actor plays three different roles. I'll be playing Tom, a straight guy who knows it all, Phyllis, an upper Manhattan socialite, and Leslie, a sexually ambiguous therapist."

Early Afternoon

There is no time for lunch. I have to go directly from class to a commercial audition. It's a cold reading, which means the actors are not allowed to preview the material. Each candidate has to read it cold. I've come to like cold readings. They more or less place all the applicants on a level playing field.

Having filled out the sign-in sheet, I wait in the director's studio, and look around at all his stuff—movie posters, memorabilia, trophies, toys. It all perfectly reflects the creative life of a director.

Over my head, a rope extends diagonally from one corner of the room to the other, like a clothesline. It's a ceiling ornament. A little monkey, propped on a bicycle, rides across this tightrope, like a circus performer. He wears a yellow tee shirt that reads, "Curious George."

Hey! I know you!

A beefy guy in a police uniform, presumably another actor, steps out of the office. Actors usually have day jobs, unless they hit it really big. God, I'd love to be a full time actor.

The director calls me in, shuts the door and says, "Okay, Derek, let me explain the shot. It's very simple. There's no dialog. Without getting into the plot, let's just say you're watching your favorite television show and the hero of the story, whom you love, gets shot. You're completely and utterly devastated. Traumatized actually. Got it?"

I nod, indicating that I understand. "Okay," he says, "I need to see you cry."

Eiffel Tower on its Side

April 23, 2006

Morning

My friend Sue has prepared a spread of omelettes, salad and French toast for breakfast. Sue has a dream apartment—the entire upper level of a house in Lanikai—steps from the ocean.

Peter, a friend of Sue's from Los Angeles, is with us. He moves to sit at the table, notices something missing, and darts off to the kitchen. Sue says, "Derek, a year ago, you did a reading for me and I asked you about where I'd buy my first house. You told me you saw grapes. Do you remember that?"

"No. I almost never remember what I say in readings. Psychic visions are like dreams, easily forgotten."

"Well I'd been thinking I'd like to get something here in Hawaii, but my friend told me about this condo for sale on Martha's Vineyard in Massachusetts. I thought, Derek said grapes, so this must be it. I feel like it's right for me, but I don't know. What do you think?"

"Well grapes certainly are a symbol of Martha's Vineyard. I'd take it as an inviting sign."

"It seems so. But it's such a big decision. I want to get it right."

Peter returns from the kitchen and places a bowl of grapes in the center of the table. Sue and I burst out laughing. Peter looks at us questioningly, and says, "What'd I do?"

I reply, "Something very magical Peter." Psychic symbols are deceptively simple, and quite efficient. Grapes are a symbol of abundance, luxury and health. Appearing as they have at this moment confirms their significance as a sign.

After breakfast, I help Sue with the dishes. As I carry our plates to the kitchen, I notice a key chain ornament lying on a side table. It's a little replica of the Eiffel Tower. Sue must have gotten it on her recent trip to Paris. Her little Eiffel Tower is lying on its side!

"Eiffel Tower on its side!" I exclaim.

"What are you talking about?"

"I did a psychic drawing exercise a couple of weeks ago, and I drew that! How bizarre."

"Maybe Paris will have a terrorist attack," Sue offers.

"No. No, that's not why I tap into this stuff. Not to pick up on terror threats. It must have some other significance. I'll have to think about it."

Afternoon

I want to step onto a bigger stage, both with my psychic work, and my acting, but New York is such a big leap. I've wanted to move there for some time now, but haven't been able to save enough money for an apartment. Plus I'll miss my friends if I leave Hawaii. Maybe I'd stall on moving even if I had the money.

The number of clients coming to me for psychic readings has increased, but an apartment in New York is not going to be cheap. My psychic class has been profitable. And what little acting I have done has helped my moving fund.

Ken, my Chinese boyfriend, has already moved to New York. I'll *have* to move if we're going to stay together. Ken has a degree in finance. Since New York is a financial center, moving there makes sense for him. He's been sleeping on a friend's couch, in a small apartment in the East Village. He's going nuts without his own space. Our plan is for Ken to find an apartment for the two of us.

Ken and I talk nearly every day on the phone. He asks, "When I look for an apartment, how I will know I found the right place?"

"You'll know. Don't take an apartment you feel ambivalent about, Ken."

"What's ambivalent mean?"

"It means, uh..." How can I say this? "Mixed feelings, or like you are not passionate. You have to love the place, and have no question in your mind that it's the right one. I admire you Ken. I'm rooting for you to find us a great apartment. I think you can."

"Can you use your psychic vision to see the right one?"

"Let me try. I can ask for a clue, some symbol to guide us. Hold on." I close my eyes and see a circle with a bunch of colors inside it. "Look for a round church window," I say. I remember a round church window, in one of my first experiences with my spirit guide.

"Okay, I'll look for it."

"Ken, I'm sure there are round church windows everywhere, but this would probably be prominently placed, like across the way, or next door."

Evening
Donna, one of my psychic students, greets me excitedly as I exit the theater's backstage door. She's brought along a friend, with whom I'm unfamiliar.

"We really enjoyed you, Derek!"

"Thanks for coming, Guys!"

"She didn't know the woman character was you," Donna says, pointing to her friend. "I didn't tell her you'd be playing three roles."

Donna's friend exclaims, "I was so surprised!"

"You didn't recognize me under those nylons and the wig?"

"You really looked like a woman!"

"Hey, now I'm insulted!"

We laugh for a bit and say goodnight.

On my way to the car, I think about how good it feels to make people laugh. *Spirit, thank you for this opportunity!*

My car is parked on the street, quite far from the theatre. As I approach it, I notice the car in front of mine has its hood up. A woman peaks out from under the hood and, upon seeing me, calls out, "Excusez moi! My batterie!" She's young, in her twenties, and French apparently. It's so rare to see a French person in Hawaii, at least this far from the hotels in Waikiki.

Her battery's dead. I tell her, "I have cables!" I have no idea how to hook them up, but I'm sure the instructions are on the box. I turn my car around, bringing the engines together.

Side by side, we lean over the girl's battery, trying to figure out how the connections work. If I were straight, I'd be very interested in her. Her ass is—Oh My God! *The Eiffel Tower!*

French Girl has the same Eiffel Tower key chain that Sue had. It's hanging out of her pants pocket *exactly sideways*! I exclaim, "The Eiffel Tower! On Its Side!"

"Huh?"

"It's..." I'm pointing, in amazement, at her pocket as if I just won the lottery.

"Yes..." She smiles, returning to the car, unsure of what to make of my little outburst.

We manage to get her car started without electrocuting ourselves. I remove the cables and, nearly in unison, we each close our respective hoods. She reaches into her pocket, pulls out her keys, and removes the Eiffel Tower. She says, "Ere, you can ave eet, as thanks."

A wonderful, yet eerie feeling washes over me, not unlike the feeling I had when the street guy in New York told me he loved me.

Driving home, I look down at my new keychain in amazement. What brought this French girl, with the Eiffel Tower On Its Side, and myself together? Is psychic visioning seeing destiny in our future or is something else happening?

I'm beginning to have this crazy idea that my Inner Guide is demonstrating how it's possible to call things and have them come to me, as if I can turn a magnet on inside me and whatever I set my mind to comes into my life. Maybe I am going to *it* instead of *it* coming to me. But either way, what a powerful concept! I love being a student of this stuff!

Seaweed

January 25, 2007

Late Morning

Recently, I've wondered if I have the ability to offer medium readings. Mediums channel the spirits of loved ones who have past from their client's lives. In meditation, I suggested to my spirit guide that if he sent me a client who asked me to serve as a medium, I'd see it as a sign I could do it.

I guess I got my wish.

The woman in front of me is about forty. She is beautiful, in an ordinary way, with a few gray hairs. She looks tired, like she is fraying at the edges. There is an air of depression about her. I can tell she is carrying a heavy emotional load.

When she made the appointment with me, she asked if I was a medium. I told her I had no experience as such, but that I would give it a try. She still went ahead with the appointment.

She opens the session with, "My son was murdered a year ago."

Oh, no. I'm in way over my head.

She has a great deal of trouble saying these words. She's still in the process of accepting this tragic turn in her life, even one year later. I feel terribly for her.

"He was 18 years old," she adds. "He somehow got in the middle a drug deal. I'm looking for some peace. Can you contact my son in the spirit world? Can you find out if he is okay? I wonder where he is...if he's moved on..."

I feel my spirit guide's presence now, and while I should be grateful that he's with me, it's more truthful to say that I'd rather strangle him. *Couldn't you have sent me an easier case? Like somebody's kindly old grandmother?*

No answer. *That* doesn't surprise me. My client looks across the table at me like a little lost dog. There is no backing out now. I have to do it.

I sit quietly in my chair for a few moments, staring into the black void behind my eyelids—seeing nothing. Not only can I not see anything. I can't feel anything either. Or hear anything. I begin to panic—I won't be able to help her.

No, he *has* to be here. He *has* to be.

I realize I've been unconsciously swaying, back and forth in the chair. The more I observe it, the more I become captivated by it. A smile, which I've only now become aware of, has come across my face.

How curious! It must be relevant. Everything we experience is relevant. I have nothing else to claim I am experiencing of her son. So I enquire within about it. Why am I swaying like this? What else do I feel?

Water. I am in the ocean! I'm swaying with a gentle tide, back and forth. As soon as this realization comes to me, a wave violently washes over my body in my mind—WHOOSH!

I am flattened and tumbled about. My imaginary body is thrown forward wildly. Then, as the waters of the wave flow backwards, I am thrown back. WHOOSH! Though the wave is forceful, the water kind of tickles, like it's massaging my back.

The water's movement becomes gentle again, as does my swaying, back and forth. Presumably, this will only last until the next big wave comes. In my mind I call out, "Boy!" She never gave me his name. "Are you in the ocean?"

"Yes!" he calls. Then he adds, "You are inside of me."

"Inside of you? What do you mean, inside of you?"

"I have returned to life, as seaweed."

WHOOSH! Another wave washes over me and I am again thrashed about. "Seaweed!" I yell, over the sound of the wave. "You *have* to be joking! Boy, your mother is here. She is very distressed, and you want me to tell her you've reincarnated yourself as *seaweed*!?"

"Yes!"

WHOOSH! I am thrown backwards again and tumbled about.

As the waters calm and I return to a gentle sway, I consider my predicament. This lady will want her money back if I tell her that her son has come to me reincarnated as a seaweed plant. I can't see this information helping her at all. She'll need grief counseling for years if she hears this.

"Listen," the boy calls out to me. "I love the ocean. I am most at home here. I was never really one for people, and I needed some simplicity, to just go with the flow. Here I live in harmony with nature, the rhythms around me. I am happy in this life. It is not forever, but this is healing for me. Will you tell her that?"

I open my eyes to find my client looking at me in an expectant manner. Her eyes are all watery, and suddenly I become aware that my own eyes are full of tears. But they are tears of joy.

"Your son!" I say, in a joyous sob. "He has returned to life as seaweed!"

To my spirit guide, I privately think: What a fool you make of me! "He says he is happiest in the ocean," I continue. "He needed to experience a simple life. He couldn't return to the kingdom of people just yet. He says he needs time."

Sure enough, the woman bursts out in a fit of sobs. She will probably walk out on me. I won't blame her. She says, "You have no idea how much sense that makes."

"It *does*?"

"Yes. It makes total sense. From the moment he was able, there wasn't a day that went by in my son's life that he didn't get in the ocean. He practically lived there. He was a surfer and the ocean was where he escaped. He had trouble making friends and never related well with people, with his father especially. Thank you. You have given me such peace."

I'm amazed. Thanks for the magical ride, Guide! But I think I'll skip the medium work. It's too emotional for me.

Cherry Street

March 15, 2007

Late Morning

Leaving my house, I see a guy from my neighborhood waiting alone at a bus stop across the street. We've never met, but I've seen him around a lot. The bus could take nearly an hour, so I stop and offer him a ride down the mountain.

As he gets in my car, he sees a book about learning Japanese on the back seat. He thanks me for the ride, and then says, "Oh, you're learning Japanese. You got a Japanese girlfriend?"

That's an interesting conclusion to arrive at based on the evidence. Being gay, I always have to think about how to respond to questions like this. I figure, if someone's asking, why should I hide? On the other hand, it's none of his business.

In the moment it takes me to consider telling him I wouldn't have a girlfriend, he says to me, "Wait. I'm talking to a friend."

He has one of those tiny cell phone pieces clipped around his ear. Returning to a phone conversation he'd apparently been having with someone before he got in the car, he shouts, "What? He's *gay*? Ha!"

Who arranged this coincidence!?

I've been reading about the archetype of the trickster lately. The trickster is a personality within us, whose primary function is to keep the ego in its place. The trickster reminds us to laugh because laughter opens our minds and frees us from rigid preconception.

Maybe it was my inner trickster who suggested I offer this guy a ride.

The guy continues his phone conversation for most of the drive down the hill. Once he finally gets off the phone, he seems to forget the question he put to me. I let him off at a public transit connection point downtown and continue on my way.

I stop at a sandwich shop, and, as I review the menu board, a middle aged Filipino guy takes a step towards me and says, "Derek! Remember me?" I vaguely recognize him. "I sold you fruit when you used to have your ice cream business." I try to place him, but I can't. God, my memory is going.

"Hi. Yes, I remember." Liar! "It's great to see you!" It seems like he's from another lifetime. And I truly *don't* remember this guy, except I know I really liked him. I do remember his integrity, and his genuine spirit. Funny how character shines through in memory, above everything else.

"I saw your sitcom on TV, dude! The one on Oceanic Cable."

"Oh! The Tide is High. Yeah, that was fun."

He carries on without interruption. "I didn't know you were an actor. That was cherry!"

Mid-Afternoon

The guy in front of me is in his thirties, probably second or third generation Japanese. As soon as I sit down with him, I close my eyes and see a cherry. It comes to my imagination in a simple outline; the typical shape of a cherry placed on top of an ice cream sundae. Psychic impressions are often simple, like road sign symbols.

I am currently performing in Chekov's The Cherry Orchard. So my first reaction to seeing the cherry is to dismiss the vision as bleed-through from my own experience. And now that I think of it, the guy at the sandwich shop just used the word. It's definitely some sort of contamination from my own life's experience.

For about twenty minutes, I leave him insights drawn from my personal collection of eclectic postcards. I've long stopped using the traditional tarot. Those images are classic—knights on horses, chariots, people stabbed with swords—but my clients can't relate to them. The postcard images I've collected are more modern. They're of people, places and things from around the world, which I use like a regular tarot deck.

I see an old woman on one of the cards and think of my client's grandmother. And as I do, the cherry symbol returns in my imagination. I ask, "Is your grandmother still alive?"

"Yes."

"You know how people say something is cherry and they mean that it's special?"

"Yeah."

*"Well, that expression doesn't seem like it's from your grandmother's time, but I hear her saying it."

"My grandmother's name is Cherry."

"Really? That's her name?"

"Yes. It's Cherry."

My goodness! I'm still learning to sort through what in my mind is a psychic impression, and what is not. I look down at some cards I've laid out on the table. On one, a suitcase catches my eye. On another, I see a picture of the world. These two images compel me to ask, "You have a trip coming up?"

"Yes."

I see the cherry in my imagination again. Where in the world are cherries famous? Japan comes to mind. The cherry blossoms are quite famous there. But cherry blossoms are also famous in Washington D.C. In fact, I think the Washington D.C. trees came from Japan. *It's one or the other, Derek. Take a stab at it.* I ask, "You're going to Japan?"

"Yes, I am! In two weeks."

Late Afternoon

My friend Steven calls asking if I want to see a movie. We decide on Zodiac, a thriller set in San Francisco about a real life serial killer. An hour into the movie, we're shown a reenactment of a Zodiac murder. It takes place at the intersection of *Washington and Cherry* streets.

A knowing runs through me. The symbol, Cherry, is talking to me. A coincidence like this, it has to be. Mentally, I leave the movie for a few moments, looking for the thread.

I'm currently acting in a play called The Cherry Orchard. A guy refers to my sitcom as "cherry." So this could be about acting or performing. I read for another guy who is going to Japan, presumably, in part, to see his grandmother, named Cherry. The Washington Cherry trees were gifts from Japan, so there's some sort of Japanese American connection. I see Cherry in a film in such a way that it ties directly to my reading.

Out of all this, two suspicions stir within me: *I will work professionally in film. And I will go to Japan.*

Maui Moon

May 30, 2007

It's midnight on Maui and I'm feeling lucky. A full moon illuminates a cobalt blue sky. I pass silhouetted palm trees as I drive along the shoreline road to Lahaina. To my left, the ocean sparkles, frosted with an iridescent sheen of silver light. I stop the car, and get out, just to take the scene in. "God, my life is beautiful!"

In Lahaina, a table is set up for me on the patio of the Hard Rock Cafe where I'm to do psychic readings for high school graduates. The place is teeming with over-excited seventeen-year-olds. They're like popcorn kernels over a hot fire: ready to explode at any moment.

As soon as I sit down, five kids cram themselves into three seats placed at my table. "The psychic!"

Two rows of bystanders look on from behind. Talk about pressure! I scream over the music to a boy seated opposite me, "What's your name?"

"Kekoa!" He's a good looking kid.

"You have a girlfriend who's crazy about you." Kekoa smiles proudly. "She's ready to marry you but you're not willing yet, right?" He's still smiling. "Because it's not time. Be honest with her. You're too fond of getting into trouble, Kekoa."

"Wow, you pretty good!"

"You know the difference between right and wrong, but choose wrong anyway. I see another woman you'll probably meet soon, older than you. Her scene isn't good for you. She's involved in some bad things. Walk away or you'll get pulled into her drama. I see you working around law enforcement."

"Damn! You see jail!?"

"Jail? Well, actually, yeah, like a correctional facility? Maybe for boys who get into trouble. But I see you counseling them, helping them rehabilitate themselves or get jobs."

"I have a court hearing next week. It's not going to go good, is it."

Oh, my God, this kid. "Kekoa, I think this chapter of your life is about learning to make good choices for yourself, and what life is like 'on the inside.' Once you're out, and older, I see you as a social worker, helping the kids inside. You're too smart to be getting into this kind of trouble."

A girl standing behind Kekoa calls out, "What happens to the girl who loves him? Does she get to keep him?" Looking up at her, I see she has tears streaming down her face.

It's the girlfriend! I don't say anything. My face conveys my answer— probably not. She runs away crying and Kekoa goes after her. I feel like I'm in a 2007 version of Grease.

A boy named Josh sits down. "Josh, you're well liked. I see you as a networker, a politician. I'm going to share a psychic scene I see of your future, okay?"

“Okay.”

“I see you as a producer, perhaps in the entertainment industry, or at least around famous people. Your friends will be jealous. I hear one of them saying, "You got to meet *Steven Spielberg*?"

Josh smiles, and I think to myself, honestly Derek, where do you get this stuff? I ask, "What do you want to do with yourself, Josh?"

"I'm going to a screenwriting school in L.A."

"Oh! Well I guess you're going to make it big then, huh? Remember us little people!"

"What about me?" calls out a pretty girl by his side. "Am I going to get married?" I turn to Josh. "Is she your girlfriend?"

"Hell, no!" They all laugh.

"Just checking." I consult my imagination and see a really fat man on a horse. The horse he's on is buckling under his weight. I don't know how to frame this insight with the girl. "Yes...there's a guy here," I say, stalling. "I believe you will get married."

"Is he fat?" a boy above her calls out, jokingly.

Amazing. If people only knew how psychic they are, they’d explore that frame of mind more. "You're very intuitive," I reply to the boy. "Actually, yeah, he is kinda big."

A roar of laughter. The boy screams, "Ha, Shawna!"

"He's a good guy, Shawna. The real tried and true kind." Shawna's facial expression tells me she is pleased by this prospect. "He'll make you very happy. I see you being particularly knowledgeable about food and health."

"Ooh!" She cries out. I want to study food science and nutrition!"

I nod in agreement, turn to the next girl and ask, "What's your name?" And as I do, I think, How great is *this*! I'm planting seeds under a full moon on Maui.

Japanese Dragonfly

July 24, 2007

Morning

Leaning over the railing of the fourth-floor balcony of my Tokyo hotel, I reflect on the sixty psychic readings I've done over the last few weeks. Was I relevant? Uplifting? Did I help?

You have to trust, Derek.

I take a deep breath, and sigh at the strangeness of it: Me, in Japan, doing psychic readings.

Turning to my right, I see a dragonfly land on the railing a foot and a half away from me. For a few moments, I admire her sparkling-green body glitter. Through huge fly-like eyes, she says to me, "Dream big, my friend."

Don't you worry, *I'm dreaming!* I'm in *Japan* for crying out loud.

She glances over to a honeybee twirling in circles a few inches beside her, and suddenly I am transported to a dream I had last night in which my face was covered with a gentle swarm of bees. In it, I feared I would be stung if I opened my eyes, but slowly I did open them and was amazed to see skyscrapers all around me completely covered in bees.

That's Tokyo—twelve million busy bees.

Dragonfly stays for a couple of minutes, batting her blue and purple iridescent wings at me. Finally, she takes off, vertically, and I think of her inspirational role in human flight technology. A visit from Dragonfly means magic is afoot.

Early Afternoon

I am granted my request for a window seat on the upper deck of a Japan Airlines 747. There is a smaller cabin upstairs and consequently, better service. Due to the curved configuration of the plane, when you sit by the window, you get the added benefit of a wide windowsill on which to place your things.

I always thought the upstairs compartment was reserved for first class. I asked a friend (who's had several passports stamped) if she knew you could sit upstairs with a coach ticket and she said she didn't even know planes *had* upper decks. *This is the best kept secret!*

As the plane pulls away from the gate, four JAL baggage handlers on the tarmac below stand at attention, bowing and waving at the passengers. *Only in Japan.*

Hey, I'm flying international. Free drinks! "Do you have American whiskey?" I ask the perfectly cloned flight attendant. Furrowing her eyebrows, she checks the cart. "We have this," she says, holding up a bottle of twelve-year-old single malt, as if it wouldn't do. *How nice!*

Dinner comes. I am served raw salmon on potato salad with a tofu pate. Cold salad of kobacha squash, with beets, confetti of bell peppers, edamame beans and an onion dressing. Bordeaux wine.

I have to write this down! I pull out a pen and start writing the dinner menu on the back of my chop stick wrapper. *What a dweeb.* The guy two seats over glances sideways at me. Who's the airline food critic?

Flank steak with carrots, ginger, onions, and egg over rice. Panna cotta with caramel sauce and shaved chocolate. Hot green tea.

Look at this; there are 300 of us, each with a TV, we're flying at 39,000 feet, eating *this*. What a feat for humankind! Tokyo to Bangkok in five hours! Did anyone imagine this a hundred years ago?

Yes, Dragonfly. I'm learning to dream big.

Cambodian Dragonfly

July 28, 2007

Early Morning

I am a sardine, packed with forty other tourists into what looks to be an old airplane fuselage that has been converted into a water bus. We are moored along a decrepit dock at Phnom Penh.

Having laid claim to seats 1A and 1B, my friend Michelle and I sink low into our seats, and hide behind our sunglasses and books. We're hoping none of the other passengers will realize their tickets have been issued with seating assignments. We are supposed to be seated *much* farther back—closer to the smelly toilets.

In twos and threes, the tourists enter with their backpacks. Ducking their heads, they squeeze their way through the starboard escape hatch, scan the length of the dismally cramped fuselage, frown in despair, and make their way to the back.

Keep moving tourists. You're not sitting here. These are ***our*** *seats.*

It's a six-hour boat ride to the Temples of Angkor. The boat captain tells us the river is low. He'll have to drop us off seven kilometers from town. Apparently, a motorcycle taxi will take us the rest of the way. Every moment is a mystery in Cambodia.

We spent months romanticizing this Southeast Asian backpacking trip. The reality is a bit of an adjustment. Turning to Michelle, I ask, "Is this the Mekong?"

"No," she replies. "It's the Tonle Sap." We gaze out at the brown water. Last night, after smiling through a Cambodian specialty dish called (truly) Fish Amok, we took a long walk along the riverbank. Phnom Penh looked like it had just endured a bombing campaign. None of the buildings were finished. Many were crumbling.

Now, as we pull out of the dock, I ask Michelle, "Didn't we bomb Phnom Penh in the Vietnam War?"

"The war was with Vietnam, wasn't it? Why would we do that?"

"I don't know. I hear Nixon saying Phnom Penh." We each laugh, feeling shame at our ignorance of history.

Late Morning

Wakening from a sleep, I run my fingers across my lip, checking for drool. Houses on stilts line the river. Through the window, Michelle takes pictures of children playing at the water's edge. We see women washing clothes and men fiddling with their boats.

I have to go to the bathroom. I make my way to the back of the cabin, pry open the flimsy bathroom door and hold my breath. At my feet, brown river water is pumped continuously into a metal bowl. On the other side of the wall, the boat's engine runs full-throttle, causing the back of the boat to vibrate vigorously. As I inhale molecules of urine, wood varnish and exhaust fumes, I pee straight into the river.

Upon returning to my seat, I ask Michelle, "Do you think Phnom Penh has a sewage treatment facility?" She rolls her eyes over to me sideways and looks down. No.

"We're not eating any more fish, Michelle."

As the boat barrels up the river, I slip through the escape hatch in search of better air. Scaling a nine-inch ledge with no railing, I creep my way along the side of the boat, clinging for dear life against a strong headwind. A fellow traveler offers me a helping hand and pulls me up onto the roof. Six others have made the journey. Some of them are sprawled out with their shirts off, sunbathing.

The river widens and before long we're in a vast sea of brown. The water must be fairly shallow because we often pass through small patches of plants.

A dragonfly invariably attends each of the little plant pods. The farther we travel up the river, the more I notice them. Apparently the dragonflies live on the water!

Up ahead, two guys on a small boat are flagging us down. In a bit of maritime courtesy, we pull up to their boat to pick them up.

In the meantime, a dragonfly lands on a railing two feet from me. As we resume our journey and pick up speed, the boat naturally begins to vibrate. I expect the dragonfly to spring off, but she keeps hanging on, even as the wind picks up.

"What are you teaching me, Dragonfly?"

She is clinging on for dear life, buckling down against an onslaught of intensifying headwinds. Before she can answer, or perhaps *as* an answer, she finally releases her grip and I watch as she is swept away in a tornado of exhaust fumes. She tosses and tumbles for a bit, then regains her bearings.

She looks angry, like an agitated bee. She fixates on me and shouts, "*Gratitude*!"

The Big Dream: The Big Apple

I Love New York

October 10, 2007

I turned forty last month, and *finally* moved to New York. If life is a play, I'm an actor in the role of my dreams.

In New York, of course, there are churches everywhere, and round windows commonplace in them. When I first arrived and saw the apartment Ken found for us, I couldn't believe how prominently the round church window I had psychically envisioned was featured in our view. We look *directly* at it through our living room window!

Fifty yards from my doorstep on West 81st street, I see a bright yellow balloon tied to a tree. In big black letters, it reads "Oz". Stepping closer, I see "The Wizard of" printed within the O. It's a clever bit of marketing from a moving company located nearby. The company byline reads, "Because there's no place like home."

Instantly, I have flashbacks of two past coincidences: one, of the song Somewhere Over the Rainbow being whistled on the street, and the other, of The Boy From Oz moving to New York. Seeing the word Oz, with its message printed on the balloon like this, gives me a warm feeling.

Recently, in a psychic reading for my friend Michelle, I offered her the number fourteen as a guiding symbol. She called me a few days later and said, "I don't understand how fourteen is going to mean anything to me." I said, "Don't worry, you'll know. It'll show up in such a way that it matters."

"Like where?"

"I don't know! Like an address or something. But it can't mean anything if you don't *look*!"

I have no doubt at this point that numbers are intelligent. I already experienced that with 1040. Fourteen certainly could "coincidentally" appear in Michelle's life in such a way as to hint at a message. But before she could even interpret what the number might mean, she would have to notice it. The number would have to leap out at her, and appear in a place relevant to some question she is asking of life.

Maybe there's more to it than me telling Michelle to look. The number can't communicate with her if she doesn't believe in it.

It's hard to imagine that a psychic symbol of any value would just be made up on a whim. But some of my most accurate psychic visions have come with the feeling that I've made them up. Who knows the source of any given idea anyway? Why should a spontaneously made-up thought carry any less weight than one that has been deliberated upon?

Numbers have a symbolic meaning all their own, but it's the symbols they interact with, and the places they appear that will most likely reveal a message.

There are a million places to study acting in New York. I've had no idea which ones are right for me. Two people recommended One On One Productions to me, so I've decided to give them a try. I'll have to audition to get accepted and if I get accepted I'll not only get great training, I'll also get access to some of the top casting directors and agents in film and television.

I prepare two monologues and head down to the place. While waiting in the green room I pick up a tri-fold brochure they have laid out on a table. It reads, "One On One Productions has been opening doors for actors for fourteen years." I open the flap and read, "Our classes are limited to fourteen students so you can get the individual attention you deserve."

I don't know how much more obvious the number fourteen could be! Opening doors. Individual attention. Fourteen certainly seems to imply this would be a great place for me to study!

Number 14

October 17, 2007

"Stop!"

My heart is pounding from terror. Ken, who was driving our car at high speed, ran a red light. We were nearly killed. Our back bumper passed within inches of a crossing truck. I was screaming at him from the passenger seat. "Stop!"

I know I heard myself scream in my dream mind. Yet now that I am awake and upright in bed, I'm wondering if I actually said it aloud. How relieved I am to be in the safety of my reality! Our near accident was only a dream.

As I record all this in my psychic diary, I realize that we weren't just driving anywhere. My dream mind chose route fourteen, a turnpike passing through the town where I grew up. The number fourteen is still communicating with me.

As I read through my psychic diary, I become aware of how prominent a role dreams have played in my psychic journey. I've relied upon my dreams to help me understand the nature and perspective of my psychic mind. The dream mind and the psychic mind are pretty much the same.

I want to stretch with this dreaming/psychic mind, see what it can do. It can see through time, as we perceive it. I've witnessed that. Can it go to another decade as well as next week? Where does the psychic mind choose to go? Why does it go there? What am I to do with what I've learned on this psychic journey? I have so many questions.

I ask questions with the intent to observe a reply. I've learned that when I ask a question about the workings of my psychic mind, life delivers the answer.

A few weeks ago, Gina, a friend of mine, wrote to me of a dream she'd had, in which I appeared. She wondered about the dream's possible meanings. Neither I nor Gina had any idea how psychic her dream would be for me. But dreams offer multiple layers of meaning for both the interpreter and the dreamer. The dream interpreter is also affected by the dreamer's dream.

This doesn't mean we are subject to the literal events of someone else's dream if we play a part in those events. We are merely affected by observing them. The more I've grown as a psychic, the more of an observer I've become. By declaring myself separate from the characters and events I envision, I am protected from their dream experiences, yet I can't help but be changed by them.

And I would say the same is true for my clients when they hear of my psychic visions for them. It's like watching a movie. We are not part of it, but it changes us.

Gina dreamt she brought her mom to a party I was having at my Manhattan apartment. Her dream mom wasn't her real mother. She was "a more cool, contemporary version" of her mom. I was playing a guitar, on which an increasing number of strings kept appearing. The scenery changed abruptly. My party continued, except now I was living in a "desert oasis".

Why a desert, I wondered, examining the dream? Why an alternate mom? Why me? Why the guitar and the increasing strings?

In my interpretation, I wondered if Gina was contemplating the role of motherhood and its attendant responsibilities. "Adoption," I wrote, "or even the idea of being a surrogate mother might come up for you. And if not for you then maybe someone around you." Seemed like one way to look at it to me.

A few days later, I was called to a film audition to be held at the New York Film Academy. The casting director sent me an email including directions on how to get there. In it, he wrote that I should "get off the train at 14th street." He asked me to be there at two o'clock. Two o'clock: the 14th hour.

I met the director, and he said, "I had intended to call my film Desperation, but for reasons I won't go into, I had to change it. I've decided to call it 'Arid Airs' because the atmosphere is very dry. If I select you for this film, I want you to think like you are in a desert the whole time we are filming. You would be playing the husband of an infertile woman with whom you have been married for some time. You and your wife have decided to contract a surrogate mother to have your child. This scene is between you, your wife and this surrogate mother."

I was stunned. The warm euphoria that ran through me at that moment is indescribable. Later that evening, the director telephoned to offer me the part.

During the filming, I was talking with the film's sound guy, an Indian, whom I'd learned would be creating the soundtrack. I asked, "Do you play an instrument?"

"Yes, I play a kind of guitar, except it has more strings than a regular guitar. It has sixteen strings."

I was asking the Universe about the capabilities of the psychic/dreaming mind, and the Universe provided me with an answer. In dreams, we can leap through time, but we can also enter other people's worlds, and see through their eyes. Gina's dream proves this. The adopted mother, the desert, the guitar with added strings. It's all here—*in my reality!*

Of course, Gina's dream has infinite meaning for her as well. But one implication of this idea is that we all have a certain psychic knowing of one another. The psychic mind is piercing, and can go *anywhere*.

Snake Bite

November 16, 2007

Early Morning

"I had funny dream last night."

"I had *a* funny dream last night. Don't forget the little words, Ken." Ken's English has been slowly improving.

"*A* funny dream last night," he continues. "I dream a snake bite the tip of my penis!" Ken laughs heartily at this, as do I. "I yelled out for pain," he continues, "but then, I look down and my penis, it was okay."

"That's funny, Ken."

"What do you think it means?"

"You got me. I'll have to think about that one."

Early Evening

Brent is hosting Ken and I for dinner at his Harlem apartment. "Brent, I still can't believe you're living here in New York, and twenty minutes from me at that."

"Yeah, I don't know how long I'll last in this apartment," he says, "but I like the city."

"This place *is* kinda sketchy," I say, looking around at the cracked, warped walls. There's a slight garbage smell coming in from the hall. The heat is on so high that all the tenants have their windows open. "Can't you control the heat?" I ask.

"No. I've told the landlord. It's a shame, the waste. There are cockroaches too. And the neighbors are...Oh, I don't want to go into it."

"You'll get something else," I tell him.

"It's close to Columbia, which is why I took it. And it's not expensive, comparatively speaking. I'll move to something better next year."

"Look for a Buddhist symbol, and a door chime," I tell him.

"Huh?"

"Never mind. I was suggesting some psychic symbols to follow. Call me when you want to move. If you're interested, maybe I can help you find a place."

Brent bought all the food for dinner. But it's Ken's job to cook it, as he's the one with all the cooking talent. Brent gives Ken an orientation of the kitchen and they discuss some possibilities as to how dinner might be prepared.

"You know what they say about too many cooks," I say. "I'll be perusing the living room while you guys work out dinner." I meander into the living room and look over Brent's bookshelf. Shakespeare, Moliere, Twain, Emerson. "Brent, you've got some great books!"

"Yeah," he replies, in a halfhearted way that tells me he is engaged with Ken. I see "The Hero with a Thousand Faces," by Joseph Campbell, and take the book from the shelf. I let it fall open to a random place in the middle. My eye falls to a passage about a dream interpretation Mr. Campbell offered one of his African clients. Campbell's client dreamed that a snake bit the tip of his penis!

Unbelievable! The book nearly falls out of my hands. "Ken!"

"What?" he yells. "I'm busy!" Steam is coming out of the kitchen. Pans are clanking. I can hear the two of them maneuvering around each other, urgently talking in hushed tones.

I call out, "You're not going to believe this, Ken!"

"Brent," Ken yells, "He always talk to me when I in the middle of cooking!"

I say, "Okay, fine! I'll wait."

I continue reading. Campbell apparently saw this dream as a symbol of circumcision, a rite of passage where a young man is separated from his mother and initiated into the world of men.

But what's amazing to me is that circumcision is not generally in Ken's culture. He's Chinese. But he had the same dream as this African guy, a dream which, according to this book, occurred some decades ago! Some dreams really are universal, as Carl Jung, the Swiss psychiatrist, claimed.

As I think about it, the interpretation Campbell provides of Ken's dream seems appropriate. Until recently, Ken had been financially reliant upon his mother. But now that he's graduated from college, and has a new job, he's gaining his independence. Just the other day, he was expressing to me that he can no longer ask his mother for money. I see this dream as confirmation that he's his own man.

Recently, I asked the Universe about the capabilities of the psychic/dreaming mind. Again, the Universe has responded! Ken himself asked me what I thought the dream meant after he dreamt it. Since he asked, the answer came in the form of a coincidence.

I have to *ask questions* to receive answers! This is such an important concept to remember in engaging with the psychic mind. A psychic is a channel for Spirit's messages. The answers to our questions are presented to us, if we are open to seeing them.

Everyone is psychic—Ken, the African, my friends Gina and Jim—but not everyone observes that aspect of mind. The psychic mind communicates using patterns, coincidences, or, as Carl Jung called them, synchronicities!

"Ken!" I call out. "I *have* to tell you this!"

"Not now!"

Amphibians and Reptiles

November 19, 2007

Early Morning

As I lay in bed, I wonder about a dream I had in which I was sleeping in an A-frame style house. Hornets were flying around my room, making clicking sounds as they bumped into my steeply slanted ceiling. From my dream bed, I watched them assault some really small flies in mid-air. I never felt threatened by the hornets, even though I was relatively close to them.

As always with my dreams, I am left mystified. What does an A-Frame house mean? It didn't feel like an attic. That might represent where memories are stored. And what of the hornets? They symbolize society, organization, and work. They have stingers. I'm not sure how any of this applies to my life.

Late Afternoon

On the platform of the 42nd street subway station, a man attempts to play two trumpets at once. A couple of buddies stand behind him. One has a rattle and raps at some cans, the other strums a guitar. A small boy in front of me drives a finger up one of his nostrils. With his other hand he grabs hold of the railing of the up escalator and wobbles a bit as he steps onto the first stair.

Derek, as soon as you get on that bus, you're going to rub sanitizer on your hands. Since moving to New York, I confess to becoming a little obsessed with cleanliness. I always carry hand sanitizer in my pocket. Germs are everywhere!

The escalator is broken. Whenever I step onto a stationary escalator my body behaves as if I just returned to earth after a month in outer space. Gravity seems to double. So established is it, in my mind, that the stairs of an escalator move, that when they are not in motion, I can't seem to walk on them with the same pressure I would on immobile stairs. Why is this!?

I sense there is some message for me in this mental trickery, perhaps something about mind-body coordination or illusion. I often have this feeling that the Universe is reaching out to me, trying to communicate something, but I'm only getting one part of a larger message.

I'm heading to Rhode Island, to my parent's house, my childhood home. The seat next to mine on the bus is unoccupied, so I spread myself out. We leave the terminal and the bus makes its way through the surly traffic. As we leave the city, I get sleepy.

It begins to rain intermittently, hard enough for the driver to turn on the large windshield wipers. The view of grey skies and muddy fens out of my window looks like a Monet painting.

A smiley woman in her forties with long auburn hair and a shiny face appears on a small television monitor to thank us for traveling with her bus company. In a strong New Jersey accent she intones, "Yoah safety is auh numba one concean. Yoah seat reclines back so you can ride in comfoat."

A teenager across from me is absorbed with his media player. The bus driver wears a headset over his ears. I imagine him to be listening to some instructional CD on how to trade currency from your own home. The woman continues, "Use yoah cell phone only in an emeagency." The drone of the bus's engine has a hypnotic effect on me, and I become sleepier. "The tempaotua has been set for yoah pleaszha. If foa any reason you ah transported to the futua, you will be comfortably sedated so you can accept the realady of the situation around you...Peel the backing and apply to yoah temples, the bus terminal is yoah final destination..."

Evening
"Did you know the White Pine bears cones only every other year?" my mother says, over pork chops and mashed potatoes. "Dad and I noticed our White Pine didn't have any cones one day and thought it strange, so we looked it up. Thirty-five years we've been here, and we never noticed the cones don't come every year on that tree! Can you believe that? Nature provides us with endless discoveries right in our own back yard! I am continually in awe of it."

When my mother makes statements like this I see where I got my sense of wonder and curiosity. I'm grateful for it.

After dinner I work on my computer for a few hours. I begin to feel tired, and head to bed. As usual, I feel like a giant entering my childhood bedroom. I have to duck my head around the edges of the room where the ceiling slants with the shape of the roof. My mother calls up to me, "We don't turn the heat on upstairs! I put an electric blanket on the bed for you!"

"I'll be fine. Thanks. Good night."

I stay up a bit reading Camino Real, Tennessee Williams' surreal tale of people trying to escape life in a small desert town. A few ladybugs, attracted to my light, clack and click on the ceiling above me.

Here's my dream! The bugs, the slanted ceiling, me on the bed. The bugs aren't hornets and the house isn't an A-frame, but these elements are similar enough to my dream for me to see the dream as psychic. I previewed the future.

My psychic dreams never quite match my subsequent reality though. My mind alters things a bit. It sees a version of the future. Can I train myself to dream a more precise copy of the future? I wonder what I would learn if I studied how my psychic mind's visions differ from reality.

Late Night
I'm in a laboratory. The lights are turned off. A boy taps my arm excitedly, and waves me toward him. "Come here," he whispers secretively, pointing to a terrarium. "Look at this!" All is dark around us, except for a bluish white light that comes from the terrarium.

In the center of the glass box sits a rattlesnake, staring at me. Its body is perfectly coiled. Its head is poised erect, about five inches above its body.

The boy goes around to the other side of the terrarium, where a cartoon frog has been painted on the glass. The frog's eyes are not filled in. They're formed by large circles of unpainted glass. It makes for a painted mask. Placing his face right up to the glass the boy wears the mask of the frog. From my side of the terrarium I watch him, as the frog, blink at me.

I laugh at his game and press my nose and lips to the glass on my side of the terrarium. The snake between us seems unimpressed. I make like a sucker fish and kiss the glass, looking past the snake at the boy/frog.

With lightning speed, the snake strikes at my face, hitting the glass with a thump. I leap back in shock. Shit, that scared me!

I feel a bit foolish for having been tricked into moving my head when the terrarium's glass was clearly there to protect me from the snake. *Try it again, Snake! I dare you!* I touch my nose to the glass again, and again the snake strikes. Though the glass is there to protect me, again I shiver and yank my head back in fear. I can't seem to get my body to trust what my mind knows.

Ssssss!

November 22, 2007

Ken and I walk up Amsterdam Avenue on the Upper West Side, looking for a place to have lunch. "Ken, what I'm saying is, on the escalator, for the first step or two, I couldn't get my body to adjust to what my mind knew. Then the idea of that experience with the escalator was mirrored in my dream with the terrarium glass. My dream mind recreated the dynamic of my body not believing what my mind was seeing— but in a different form. And, I see the terrarium as a symbol of having to work within the confines of a structure."

"Uh huh."

He's not listening. I don't blame him. What's my point? I continue on anyway, "This morning, I took my laptop to a cafe to write about my dream. I left the place, and on my way home, I passed a salon where a little boy was pressing his face flat up against the window."

"Let's go in here," Ken says, darting off into a store with birds in the window.

"Ken, I don't want to look at caged birds. Not now, please?"

"Just for a minute! Come on." Relenting, I go in with him. Instantly the smell hits me. Bird shit. Lovely.

Walking the aisles, I see they have fish tanks, too. "Hey, D!" Ken says, excitedly. "Come over here!" I walk around the fish tanks and find Ken pointing into a terrarium. "Look! A snake!"

17.

June 7, 2008

Late Morning

"I came to New York," my client says, "to pursue a career as a songwriter."

"Well, you're in the right place," I reply.

"Yeah, I feel that, definitely, but it's been so hard lately. I signed a contract with a major publishing house and have had *some* success..."

"Good for you!" A globe turns in my mind. "Abroad?"

"Uh, yeah, actually. Mostly. But things have stalled..."

"Because I think most of your success will be overseas," I say. My client frowns upon hearing this news.

"Not New York?"

"Through New York. I think you're in the right place. You write songs for pop singers? Like songs that would go on the charts?"

"I have. And I would love for one of my songs to make it onto the charts."

"I see one at number 17."

"17," she says, surprised. "Wow. That's pretty high."

"Yeah, I'd say."

"Well, where did you get this number 17 from?"

I chuckle, and say, "You question my sources?" She's not sure I'm joking. She looks at me with a...is that a smile? I add, "Seems you don't believe the number is possible."

"No, I do," she says.

"Okay."

Silence.

I continue, "How am *I* supposed to know where it came from? You're paying me to use my imagination, do you realize that?" I laugh heartily at this, because the notion still strikes me as funny for some reason. I believe in my imagination, for the most part. But a small part of me still thinks, 'What a ruse'!

"The number approached me," I explain. "I saw it with my third eye. That's all I can tell you. That, and that being in a funk, such as the one you're in now, will contribute to a song that will bring you some success." This I also declare with a confidence drawn from an unknown source. Jung refers to an "unknown knower" within all of us, a wise, unknowable part of ourselves. It's a concept I like. I haven't spoken directly to my spirit guide of late, or felt like I've witnessed him in any definable way. But I know he's there.

"It's a song that you'd never have written had you not felt this way," I add.

"Well, what does 17 mean as a number?"

"A very good question. In the system of the tarot it's The Star. I don't have to tell you what it means to be a star in music do I?"

"No."

She is smiling now. "I like to play a psychic game with numbers, because numbers are alive. They're like the alphabet of the Universe, so to speak. They seem to have a way of appearing in strategic places as if to make a point, or point the way. They're even woven into music, so maybe 17 will have a special way of appearing. Where it shows up is up to the number though. If the number 17 attracts you, why don't you ask it to communicate with you as a sign?"

Evening
Assistant director: "Quiet on the set!"

Director of photography: "Camera speed...rolling!"

Director: "Action!"

My mind is split. One part of me is me. Another, is Josh, the character I am playing. I am standing at the threshold of Angel's apartment, a ratty second floor unit, deep in the heart of Brooklyn. Angel is Josh's nephew, who is played by a guy named Jon.

As soon as the word "action" was uttered, we actors, Jon and I, entered into a dimension all our own. The "real" world outside our dimension became silent. We see it, but cannot acknowledge it.

Angel is standing about a foot into the apartment, holding the door open. I'm just outside the door, in the stairwell. We're in the process of saying goodbye. Over Jon's shoulder, I see the director of photography, perched on a stool in the corner of the kitchen. His eye is riveted to the camera. The director stands behind him with his arms crossed. The sound technician, the lighting specialist, the set designer, and others, are in the living room beyond.

The camera is a portal to the world of reality. According to the rules of the acting game, I must remain invisible to those in that world. In the world that the characters, Angel and Josh, live in, no such portal exists. They sense there are portals to other worlds, but they don't know what those portals look like.

Maybe there is an unseen camera focused on us in everyday reality. Maybe God is a writer and director, and we're all characters being played by actors we don't see. And those actors could be our spirit guides. After all, my influence on my character, Josh, will forever be a mystery to him.

This analogy implies our guides manipulate our every move, but I believe Josh is managing his moves as much as I am managing them for him. I am continually surprised, when I'm playing a character, by actions I take that I did not plan. The character seems to have free will.

Josh says, "Angel, call me if you need anything." He gives Angel a reassuring smile, and then lifts his gaze over Angel's shoulder to the kitchen wall, where one of those page-a-day calendars hangs. In a giant font, the top page displays the date Angel's father died; 17.

Déjà vu swirls around me. 17. It's from the reading I did for the songwriter. Who chose *that* date of all? Was it the set designer? The Director?

I have broken with my character. Tapping back into Josh, I realize that it may not have disclosed myself. My own confusion over the number 17 mirrors the confusion my character Josh is experiencing. He is wondering 'Why did my brother have to die on this date?' Our thought processes are nearly parallel.

In an effort to help Angel move on from his father's death, Josh points to the calendar and says, "Why don't you turn the calendar?"

I hear a ripping sound. The packing tape that holds the calendar to the wall is giving way! Little by little, all four corners of the pad peel off the wall. My jaw drops, as the book of days falls to the floor with a sharp crack.

Director: "Cut! Reset!"

German Thug

June 19, 2008

Late Morning

"Hello?"

"Hi Derek, my name is William. I'm directing the film 'Charity'. You auditioned for the role of Samuel?"

"Yes, great. Wait...which film is this again?" I've auditioned for too many to remember.

"It's about a guy who bets a lot of money on a horse and loses. He trades places with a homeless man to escape a bookie who threatens to kill him if he doesn't pay his debt."

"Oh, right. I remember. Hi."

"I had chosen another actor to play the role of the bookie, but he can't be available on the filming dates. I'm calling to see if you're interested in playing the part."

"Yes, I am!"

"I was thinking of making your character German. Can you do a German accent?"

"Yes...Ja."

"Great. I'll email you the script. I want to set up a couple of rehearsals. How's your schedule this week?"

Early Afternoon

At my computer I tsink, Hmm...dzis German accent vill be trdicky! I must rrrent some German films zo I can mimic it!

My phone rings. I answer, "Hello?"

"Derek, it's Neil. I have great news for you. Comcast is green-lighting you for their psychic show."

Hurray! Comcast approached me about a month ago with the prospect of filming a series of short psychic readings and workshops for them. I've had my fingers crossed about it ever since. I didn't want to write about the possibility of this coming to fruition for fear I would jinx it.

Sometimes, when I want something to happen really badly, I don't want to talk about it. I just want to give it my best effort, then quietly let whatever it is go, give it up to the Universe.

The Universe is like a tennis partner when it comes to things I want. I have to hit the ball—that thing I want—back to the Universe's court. I can't hold on to the ball, or the game won't be played. The Universe wants to take the ball, work its magic on it, and then send it back to me. Something happens to the ball each time it's passed back and forth.

I've read for many clients who are really upset that something in life they have wanted hasn't come true. For example, a woman who wants to get married and hasn't met the right guy; she can't hold on too tightly to what she wants, especially if she's angry about it. She has to let go, and love her life as it is. Then she will be attractive to an interested mate.

"Oh my God. Neil, I'm thrilled! Thank you!"

"It'll air on their new Paranormal TV network, as part of a series called Real Psychics."

A gentle "ding dong" from my computer lets me know William's email has come in. I ask Neil, "When will it be broadcast?" *Broadcast*. I remember that word. It was one of the first words I heard in meditation. My God, here it is, five years later. I *knew* it was important. I knew it with that inner knowing I can't quite describe. Even one word can be psychically truthful and profound.

"It'll be on air all the time," Neil says.

"All the time?"

"It's Video On Demand. Comcast subscribers can download it whenever they want. I need to set up a meeting with you. How's your schedule this week?"

Mid Afternoon

Eagerly, I open the attachment containing the script for William's film and begin reading. I'll be playing Samuel.

FADE IN TO AN APARTMENT LIVING ROOM. AFTERNOON. DAVID, mid 30's-40's, medium height, fit, slightly husky, is in limbo between sitting and jumping out of his chair. He is intently watching a horse race, shouting at his TV, while waving around a small slip of paper.

DAVID
"Come on 17! Move your ass!"

I stare at my laptop, mouth agape. *The horse's name is 17*? You've *got* to be kidding! I read on.

(FLASH BACK) BOOKIE'S OFFICE. EVENING. SAMUEL, late 30's, intimidating and tall, is sitting at a desk, talking on the phone.

SAMUEL
"...No, no, you don't understand. Right now I'm just a bookie, but if you lose, then I become a collector..."

I continue reading, fantasizing my character, Samuel, as a German thug.

"...and jou bettur be expectingk a visit rrreal quick. Because if you don't pay up, I'll keep comingk back until dzere's nothingk left to break...get dze picture?"

I LOVE this guy! I can't wait to play him!

The number 17 showed up in *two* films in which I'm playing parts. And some part of me, the Unknown Knower, seemed to know that.

Often, visions I have for my clients have shown up for me. I've thought, maybe I was only seeing my own future. But I don't think this negates the vision for my client. When a client sees me, the visions he or she gets are filtered through my mind, emotions and experiences. I saw the number 17 for the songwriter, but the fact that 17 also happened to appear for me validates the vision to me. Then again, we'll have to see, won't we?

I may never hear from that songwriter again to know if she makes the charts, but at least I've suggested the idea to her, by whatever agency. And even if my client doesn't have a number-17 song on the charts, from a symbolic or metaphorical point of view, the vision says, "Songwriter, you're a star"!

Submail!

Late at Night
Leaning sideways over the edge of the subway station's platform, I peer into the tunnel in the hopes of seeing my train's headlights. Only a few, dim track lights twinkle in the dark, black hole.

A few yards from me, a white woman digs through her purse. Farther down the platform, a black guy leans against a pillar and listens to his iPod. Along the tracks, a rat investigates a small patch of trash. The station is strangely quiet.

With a sigh, I wonder about how much my life has changed over the last few years. Or how much I've changed my life. What's different, since I identified with my psychic mind?

I live with a greater sense of gratitude. That seems to have come out of an enhanced awareness of what the Universe has to offer me, and what I have to offer for the Universe. I feel like a light's been turned on, and now I see that everything, and everyone, is connected. I've learned that I'm a channel, and everyone is a channel. That life is filled with possibilities I am probably not even capable of dreaming.

I don't feel any more powerful than before I identified as a psychic. I don't feel particularly endowed with any special talent. In fact, in the grand scheme of the Universe, I feel smaller somehow, less significant than ever. Yet, I could also say I'm a more creative designer of my life.

Psychic ability isn't about having any kind of control over anything. It's about paying attention, observing patterns in our thoughts and our reality, playing with the stuff of life.

The antenna of my psychic mind has tuned into the energies of people, numbers, insects, animals, spirits and objects. They have humorously and intelligently coordinated coincidences for me—as if to point the way. I feel as though I'm living the life of my dreams, because I'm dreaming my life!

As I continue to practice exercising my psychic mind, I'll remember to be playful. As new psychic awarenesses or capabilities unfold, I may not have a complete understanding about what I'm experiencing. I'll allow myself to be a little lost in the process, knowing that viewpoints—not necessarily answers—will come, with time. I will remain curious, imaginative and observant. And I will remember to be inspiring in my interpretation of signs and coincidences.

A sudden breeze blows out of the tunnel. A sound like a whip being cracked reverberates through the cavernous station. The train is coming.

Once the train stops, the other two straphangers and I each get into our own separate subway cars. I am the sole occupant of mine. I plop myself into a plastic seat, and as the train moves forward, an empty coffee cup rolls back and forth in the aisle. My sweatshirt will make for a decent enough pillow. I stuff it into the ledge of the window behind my head, and make myself as comfortable as I can.

The initials J.K. are etched, about twelve inches tall, into the window across from me. I stare through these into the passing wall of the tunnel. The train tips downward, speeding past graffiti. We're heading under the East river. The atmosphere feels like I'm in a suspense film.

My eyelids become weak. They're nearly closed. My eyelashes form a kind of grillwork so that so that everything I see flickers. Blue and white lights occasionally flash by.

There's an iron fence along the side of the tracks. I've never noticed that before. A bright sun pulsates rapidly between the fence's bars.

Clickety clack, a rattley rap!

Myriad stars spread out over a horizon-less black sky. Out of the corners of my eyes I see a few of the stars gather to chat. The train glides through outer space, slowing in speed.

As the fence posts pass by with diminishing frequency, the flashes of sunlight become longer in duration. I extend my hand out the window and let my fingers strum the iron fence.

The bars are softer than I would have thought, and shiny, like vinyl. They're records. Huge, vinyl records—ten times larger than the train. They're laid upright, lined up in a row, in the shape of a spiral, which goes on indefinitely.

The train stops, and I get out and stand before the curved row of disks.

With my right hand, I flip through them. Each disk is unmarked. They all look and feel exactly the same. It occurs to me that each disk contains its own universe, its own time and place. If I decide to enter one, it will take me somewhere, to another time.

I'm nine years old. I'm on a train, sometime in the past, in a car furnished with dark wood paneling and orange velvet seats. The fabric is worn in places, to a point where a course, mesh under-layer shows through.

A spider crawls tentatively on the inside ledge of the window. Just outside, a stand of craggy trees races by.

My mother sits beside me. She's putting on makeup and thinking adult thoughts. How pretty she is with her bright red lipstick and her shiny, brown hair. She looks like a movie star.

"You're awake," my mother says.

"I wasn't sleeping."

"Yes you were. Did you dream?"

"I dreamt about ice cream."

"Really? What flavor?"

"Banana!"

"Wow! Was it a banana split with strawberries and chocolate on top?"

"No. It was banana with something else, but I didn't know what it was. A lizard gave it to me. He said it wasn't just regular banana. It was *special*. And if I ate it, I could be anyone I wanted, and he showed me these three blind monkeys who were doing things with their hands."

"See no evil, hear no evil, and speak no evil?"

"I can't remember really." The train rattles on, and I squint in the light of the beautiful day.

Fields of tall grass stretch out as far as the eye can see. The grasses come in hues of yellow, green, brown and purple. The fields look like they're waving at me. I ask, "Ma, where are we?"

She smiles at me as if I asked a silly question, then shrugs her shoulders and says, "We'll be there, in due time."

Please visit my websites for the latest on my psychic and acting work!

http://www.derekcalibre.com

http://www.derekcalibre.tv

LaVergne, TN USA
11 April 2010
178907LV00004B/13/P